E Zhivindi Yag
The Living Fire

E Zhivindi Yag
The Living Fire

by Ronald Lee

Magoria Books
2009

E Zhivindi Yag · The Living Fire by Ronald Lee
formerly published as "Goddam Gypsy"

© Copyright 2009 Ronald Lee

Cover design by Sebestyén, using the image 'Flame' by Agg from
Dreamstime.com.

First Edition

ISBN 978-0-9811626-0-7

Published by MAGORIA BOOKS

www.MagoriaBooks.com

LIBRARY AND ARCHIVES CANADA CATALOGUING IN PUBLICATION

Lee, Ronald, 1934-
[Goddam Gypsy]
E zhivindi yag = The living fire / by Ronald Lee.

Previously published under title: Goddam Gypsy.
ISBN 978-0-9811626-0-7

1. Lee, Ronald, 1934- –Fiction. I. Title. II. Title: Living fire.
III. Title: Goddam Gypsy.

PS8573.E35G6 2009   C813'.54   C2009-904160-X

Table of Contents

To a Gypsy, this card portrays Mundro Salamon, the Romani ethnic hero who appears in the folk tales of the clans of Rom. He is always portrayed as a wise man, but like all men, he sometimes succumbs to temptations. He can converse with both God and the Devil whom he considers as some kind of beloved enemy. On occasion, Salamon manages to save people from the clutches and lures of the Devil by outwitting him.

Salamon stands for the peaceful philosophy of the Roma. His weapons are wisdom, cunning and superior intellect. In this he differs from non-Romani ethnic heroes. Where Achilles would dispatch his enemy with a thrust of his sword, Hornblower broadside him into driftwood and Wyatt Earp gun him down at high noon in the town square, Mundro Salamon overcomes his enemy simply by turning the greed, ignorance or carnal desires of the enemy back against him.

In this pictorial representation we see Mundro Salamon, the eternal Romanitchel, standing before the table of the magician or *magnus*. In his left hand he holds the magic wand of illusion, while his right points to the earth. This is seemingly in direct opposition to the religious beliefs of the Gypsy who sees the right hand, as the instrument of good and the left, as the instrument of evil. But as in all things, he portrays himself to the non-Gypsy in opposites, which is quite in line with the Gypsy trick of never telling his enemy the truth. As we say in Romani, "*Le Romeski shib motol o chachimos ande xoxayimos*", "The Gypsy tongue tells the truth in lies."

The balls and cups are the tools of the Gypsy trade as are the daggers through the arms, all instruments the fakir employs to bamboozle the simple.

The four hands represent the four basic races of man, white, black, brown, and yellow, that constantly reach to absorb and assimilate the elusive and eternal Gypsy. He remains aloof, a child of a former age of nomadism, long before sedentary man foolishly allowed himself to create a society in which he was either one of a privileged handful of rulers and exploiters or one of a mass of ruled and exploited.

E Zhivindi Yag
The Living Fire

The living fire is that spark of defiance that is the birthright of everyone. In some, it has gone out, in others, it is only a smouldering ember. But in a few, it blazes into an inferno of passion, creativity, rebellion and all too often, violence.

This is my story, the saga of a Canadian-born Rom. All names of characters, except mine and that of my wife, are fictitious and the drama is in places fictionalized, a parallel rather than the actuality. But the pathos, tragedy and humour are a part of my life and my struggle to find recognition and equality in the land where I was born. I failed in both of these aims and this is the story of that failure.

Ronald Lee
London, England 1970

Preface

Both Canada and the Roma have evolved in directions impossible to imagine when this novel, under its original title of *Goddam Gypsy*, was released 38 years ago! In the 1960s, Canada still basked in its image of The Two Solitudes, while in Quebec, Separatism was becoming an issue, punctuated by the local terrorism of radical elements of the FLQ and the War Measures Act in 1970. For the first time since *La Révolution des Patriotes* in 1837, armed troops would patrol the streets in *La Belle Province*.

Multiculturalism was a brand-new concept bounced around by politicians in Ottawa while Native and Women's Rights were in their infancy. Canadians in general believed that "gypsies" were either extinct or just any social dropout who wore an earring and a bandana, carried a fiddle and maybe "gypped" you as he aimlessly traveled around, rejecting the mainstream moral values of society. Many Canadian TV productions of the era simply lumped gypsies and hippies together as if the two terms were synonymous. The word Roma was unknown at that time and would remain so until after the collapse of communism and the revival of Romaphobia, dormant since the end of Nazi Germany in 1945. It rapidly resurfaced in the New Democracies after 1990 resulting in physical persecution, murder and pogroms, forcing thousands of Roma to become refugees from democracy. A few thousand soon arrived at Canadian airports seeking safety as Convention-refugee claimants.

In the 1960s, culture and the arts flourished in the Montreal subculture while the mainstream Quebec culture was undergoing the Quiet Revolution to eliminate the legacy of Maurice Du Plessis, the Darth Vader of Canadian provincial politics, who had ruled Quebec with an iron fist from 1936 to 1959, like Franco in Spain, with a brief vacation from 1940 to 1944. He was supported by the Church, the Quebec Society of John the Baptist and his *Partie Nationale*, the Quebec equivalent of Franco's fascist *Falange*. His version of Franco's *Guardia Civil*, the Quebec Provincial Police, managed to ensure political stability through unrestricted use of terror and the truncheon. In Ottawa, Diefenbaker, the last of the old Tory dinosaurs, sparred bombastically in the House with Pearson, the visionary reformist while "Pretty Pierre" waited impatiently in the wings for his chance at the throne. The computer age existed only in Isaac Asimov's Sci-Fi novels and the electric typewriter was on the cutting edge of communication technology.

Multiculturalism and Native and Women's Rights are now realities. Pearson's health care plan, Canada Pension Plan, student loans and the Maple-Leaf Flag are also realities. The Two Solitudes are being relentlessly eased, kicking and screaming, into the disposal chute of Canadian history. Separatism is falling on evermore deaf ears and the computer age is a reality. This enables us to slice through the constricting walls of theocratic mind control and political brainwashing. All of these rapid changes make it difficult for younger readers to visualize the Montreal and the Canada that I describe in the 1960s.

I left Montreal with my family for the UK after the excitement and enthusiasm of EXPO 67 when the city was in a festive mood, the best place to be in Canada at that time. I returned to find it grim and under the War Measures Act and some of my intellectual friends in jail, innocent victims of the massive paranoia and the manhunt for FLQ suspects. One well-known, outspoken, journalist associate was arrested for simply having a copy of *The History of Cubism* in his library!

The Living Fire, my rejected original title for *Goddam Gypsy*, better describes the theme of my story, a time-capsule of the Montreal subculture and life as a marginal in *La Ville Lumière* of the 1960s. All the major characters are based on real people and most of the events are based on events that actually happened. The names of characters have been changed, except mine, Yanko, which was my Kalderash name in Kolia's family and among the local Gypsies and my friends, and the events are not always in sequence. The aim was to portray the Gypsies and the denizens of the Montreal subculture as exemplified by Demitro, the local Romani spiritual elder, baffled by the rapid changes in society and struggling to lead his people into the future; Kolia, the traditional European-Kalderash Rom, trying to maintain his customs and way of life in a rapidly-changing technology; Yanko, the educated Canadian-born Rom struggling to be recognized for his ability in an uncomprehending, alien world that sees him as an interesting "gypsy" first and foremost and anything else second; Marie as the beautiful, "exotic," Native woman in a sexually-constipated, white society; Hassan, the Black Muslim, revolting against his Other-defined negro identity; Sudić, the royalist Serbian Chetnik, with his hatred of Churchill who "sold out" Mihajlovic and the Royalists to Tito's Communists; Bill, with his dream of Canada as a socialist democracy; Jilko, the Hungarian-Gypsy violinist and fish out of water; George, the off-beat journalist who aspires to be recognized as the Damon Runyon of Montreal in the closed world of an in-group dominated, journalistic and literary mediocrity where even Runyon himself would never have been recognized; Jimmy, the young Gypsy musician with his dream of becoming the "Gypsy Beatle;" and Indian George, full of venom for the anonymous white snakes who stole his tribal land.

Yanko is the link between all of these people and it was in the back yard of my flat on Park Avenue in Montreal in 1967 where they all gathered for a party on the official day of the centennial of Confederation and the massive fireworks display, to drink, smoke pot, fornicate, play music, sing and dance as the mood took them - and to incinerate the old, detested Canadian flag which had always symbolized British Canada as the puny cub of the mighty British lion. As a famous Native, rebel folk singer lit my blowtorch and happily incinerated the hated symbol of the land thieves, missionaries and whisky traders, we proudly raised the newly-authorized, official Canadian flag with the red Maple Leaf, the symbol and hope for the new concept of Multiculturalism in a new Canada yet to be created.

Today, the false image of "gypsies" as semi-mythological beings or storybook stereotypes is rapidly changing. There has been a massive influx of Romani refugees from the New Democracies and Roma (ex-gypsies) are no longer voiceless. There are an ever-growing number of Romani civil-rights and political organizations, cultural organizations, worldwide in scope and individual web sites, chat lines, bulletin boards and other accessible Internet hits produced by Roma all over the web. Numerous non-fiction books, some even by Roma, have been published about Roma in many countries and since 1993, I have been teaching The Romani Diaspora in Canada at New College, University of Toronto, as part of the Equity Studies Program, the first such course anywhere in Canada. There has been a registered Romani NGO in Toronto, The Roma Community Centre (RCC), since 1998 with another in Vancouver and since 2005, *Romani Yag*, a cultural organization in Montreal. Romani music CDs with songs in Romani are advertised on the Internet and available in many music stores. Feature films such as *Lacho Drom* and *Gadjo Dilo* portray the Roma as they are in various countries. Documentaries like *Opre Roma*, an NFB production and *Suspino: A Cry for Roma*, by Tamarin Productions of Vancouver, show the Roma in Canada, in refugee camps in Italy and in the slums of Romania. Gypsy Caravan (2007) visually portrays *The Living Fire* through Romani music and dance. Much has been done and much remains to be done. But now, in Canada, we finally have the laws and the means to do it. I have already published *Learn Romani* (2005, UK, Hertfordshire UP) and the Romani-English dictionary is now completed and has a potential publisher.

In 2009, a book like *The Living Fire aka Goddam Gypsy* would not need to be written. In 1969-70, it did! This novel tells why.

Ronald Lee
Hamilton, Canada 2009

E De Devleski, or Earth-Mother card. This is primarily the card of the dreamer, the seeker after illusions and the youth searching for the answer to the riddle of life. It also carries a warning for man not to meddle with the secret mysteries of nature which can bring either good or evil results. It is the card of the romantic, the artist, the thinker and the student, but not of the realist.

The face in the moon is Diana, goddess of nomads. The dog is the unsatisfied soul howling at the moon. The tears are the bitter tears of frustration, and the gravestone and the skull are the end of mortal existence. The evergreen tree shows the continuity of life.

This is Yanko as he sets out on his journey.

XV

I walked along the highway carrying my two suitcases. It was growing dark and I was beginning to feel lonely. My friend Alec had left earlier for Europe and Stan had driven me as far from Montreal as he could. I'd left some of my belongings with him and my ship models, research material and tools with a cousin. I had about seventy dollars in my wallet, and I figured I would need it.

I tried thumbing. But it was 1958, the beatnik era, and hitch-hikers were suspect. Finally, I got a ride with a farmer driving a truckload of pigs; he took me about thirty miles, then let me out and turned off up a side road. It was now pitch dark, except for the stream of light from transport trucks and cars on the highway. I sat on my suitcase in a field just off the road to have a smoke, and listened to the crickets and the bullfrogs. An Ontario police car passed and I realized I had left my native province behind.

I finished my cigarette and went back onto the highway. I would keep walking till I came to a motel or got another lift. I soon saw welcoming lights and found the all-night eatery still open. It wasn't very crowded, just a few truck drivers and a small group of leather-jacketed motorcycle enthusiasts. I took a table near the counter, put my suitcase underneath and ordered a meal.

I ate slowly, listening to Elvis calling his plaintive message from the jukebox.

I heard a car pull up; the door slammed and a man entered and took a stool at the bar. He interested me. He was stocky, had a thick neck and legs too short in proportion to his torso. His suit needed cleaning and his shoes, a shine. In lieu of a tie he wore a sort of ascot, and on his head a cloth cap. He was very dark, almost the colour of a Hindu and his long hair, together with the stubble of whiskers on his chin, gave him an unkempt air. His rough hands were scarred and stained. A bent cigarette dangled from his thick lips. He wore an odd looking gold ring on his left hand and had many gold teeth.

"What do you want, Mack?" the waitress asked him.

He replied in broken English trying to say what sounded to me like "two hot dogs and a cup of coffee."

"What the hell is that?" the girl said. "Can't you speak English? *I no parley the Francey.*"

"*Que le gustaria?*" I asked him, hoping he would understand.

He did, and told me that he wanted two hot dogs and a cup of coffee.

"So that's what he wants," the waitress said. "Why didn't he say so in the first place? Does he want it all dressed?"

"*Con todo?*"

"*Si, Señor.*"

I kept on eating but something made me feel nervous. I glanced up to see the man watching me in the mirror of the bar; his eyes under the wrinkled brows had a cat-look. He smiled, then got up slowly and came over towards me, his hot dog clutched in his hand like a dagger.

He sat down opposite me in the booth.

"*Con su permiso?*" he said, just before he bit off a hunk.

"I am Juanito, from Spain," he began. "Thank you for helping me to order my food. I don't speak English and nobody here understands French, Italian, Spanish, Turkish, Greek, Russian, or Arabic. Do you also speak French?"

"Je peux me défendre."

"*Bueno,* what do you do?" He glanced at my two suitcases.

I told him as best I could.

"*Un artista,*" he smiled. "You make models of old ships, *magnifico.* I've known many artists—painters, actors, dancers and musicians, all over the world. Do you have any family?"

"*Todos muertos,* both my parents are dead."

"May they sleep well," he said, seriously.

This was no Spanish idiom he'd used. I studied him again feeling that my initial guess was now justified. I looked him squarely in the eyes and asked him the question.

"*San tu Rom?*"

"*Uva,*" he replied, also in Romani, "I am a Gypsy of the Coppersmith nation. You, too, are one of us, I saw that when I came in. What are you, Rom, Sinto, Bayash?"

"My mother was a Sintaika," I told him, "my father a Machvano, a Rom of the nations like you. But my father disappeared and I was adopted by a Gazho family. I went back to live with my mother when I was fourteen. She died a year later. I've been to school and worked in offices."

He stared at me, incredulous. "*Chuda, che chorobia*—What vagaries, a Gypsy who has worked in the offices of the *Gazho. Chi mai diklem ande viatsa*—I've never seen such a thing in my life."

I found it difficult to follow his Romani. He spoke the inflected dialect of the Eastern European Gypsy clans and not the broken or half-dialects common to England and Western Europe. Romani was the first language I learned to speak, but I had forgotten much.

"Where are you going?" the Gypsy asked.

"Ottawa, Toronto, Winnipeg, I don't know."

"Why?"

"Just to go some place."

"Do you want to work with me?"

I smiled. "To do what, steal?"

"I'm a mechanic," he said, ignoring the insult. "I work all over this territory. I fix vats, I plate mixing bowls for bakeries and I service kitchen equipment for restaurants. But I need a partner who speaks English. You can teach me English and help me with the work. I'll give you a full share of whatever we make. You can still be an artist when we're not working."

I smiled at his naiveté. It had once been a wild dream of mine to go back and life with my people who still followed the old way of life in Europe. I had left one life to look for a different one, but I hadn't figured to run into a nomadic European Gypsy on the Montreal-Ottawa highway. This ought to be interesting.

"Yes, I'll work with you," I said. "Have you any family?" I knew Gypsies always live in large, extended family units.

"Yes, my father and mother live in Hull. I go home every two or three weeks for a while. Last winter we stayed in Montreal."

"What's your Gypsy name?" I asked him.

"*O Kolia le Valodiasko, hay kiro?* - Kolia the son of Valodia, and yours?"

"Ronald Lee."

— 2 —

For the next two years, I worked steadily with Kolia, job after job. Looking back now, I find they all merge and it is hard to single out specific places or details. One comes out sharper than most, perhaps because it involved Kolia's love problems. This happened in a small town near Three Rivers. I've forgotten the name of it now but it's not important, we worked in almost every town, city and village in eastern Canada back in those days.

It was the summer of 1959 and we'd gone to a motel for breakfast. Kolia had a circuit of such contact places where his customers would leave telephone messages with the manager or owner to say they had work for us. On this day there was a message from a bread and cake factory. We drove into the town about nine-thirty, through the almost deserted streets, past the church. A black-robed priest studied us paternally. Kolia made a sign of obeisance and the Father smiled pleasantly at us, opened his bible and began walking back and forth in front of his domain. We were soon past this initial danger, but now another and infinitely more ominous one forced Kolia to swerve madly and race up a side street. I had seen the cause of his alarm, two figures walking along the main street. One was tall, heavyset with a smallpox-scarred face, the other, shorter, fatter and cherub-like, with a row of ballpoints glittering in his breast pocket.

"*Arak tu bre,*" Kolia warned me as we fled, "watch out for those two. That's Zlatcho and Todero. If they find out we're here to work they'll force themselves in as partners and we'll have to pay them a full share each. Let the crooks find their own work. Those African Gypsies don't work like me; they're middle men. They overcharge and leave a bad name behind wherever they go. They were diamond smugglers in Africa."

We got to the factory by a devious route and entered the yard in the rear. Kolia parked behind a large van with the rear of the station wagon against the wall to hide the licence plates from the *Afrikaiya* should they come snooping around. We got into the factory through the garage and reached the "office" by the rickety, flour-coated stairway where we found a pretty young French-Canadian girl busy typing on an old typewriter. Kolia flashed his gold teeth and asked to see the manager in a very good imitation of the *joual* of Quebec. The girl left. Kolia nudged me and pointed to his neck, where the papal cross hung from its gold chain. It flashed in the bright sunlight in the glory of the faith. I opened my shirt to display its twin. This was *talento* in its most fundamental application.

The manager greeted Kolia like a long-lost brother.

"*Ça va, mon vieux?*" he shouted, then added something pornographic as he lunged and grabbed Kolia's testicles in a time-hallowed French-Canadian gesture of friendship. Kolia offered him an American cigarette from a special pack that he kept for such occasions, as the young secretary stood smiling nearby.

"*J'ai du travail pour toi,*" the manager informed Kolia. "*Viens t'en.*"

We followed the manager through the office and into the factory in the rear and Kolia introduced me as his assistant.

"Just over from Spain," he added, knowing that my French, though fluent might betray me as an English-speaking Canadian. Kolia, it seems, was Spanish in this particular factory and it just wouldn't do for me to be English. He had discovered that to some French-Canadians everything stupid, bad, oppressive and inhuman is centralized in one type of man, a *tête carrée*, or Englishman.

We walked through the factory and up another flour-coated stairway to the bakery where men, women and girls were busy preparing dough. A burly baker came out of the toilet, pulled up his zipper and plunged his hands into a bowl full of snow white dough, kneading it into delicate shapes as the girls gave Kolia and me speculative glances.

The head baker joined us and shook hands with Kolia who seemed to know him well. He accepted the eternal Yankee cigarette and the manager then left after telling the baker and Kolia to work out between them what work had to be done and for how much. The baker led us over to a row of medium-sized mixing bowls from which the tin-plating had worn off in certain areas exposing the bare metal underneath. There was also a pile of aluminum pots and pans burned black and covered with the incinerated remains of the former contents.

Kolia examined the basins, yelled out the price of each to me in Romani and I wrote it down on a pad.

"*Il ne parle pas français,*" he explained. "*Il parle comme une vache espagnole.*"

The baker laughed. "*Il a besoin d'une de nos filles.*"

I smiled and thought of the pretty secretary.

The total came to a hundred and sixty-five dollars. I made it a hundred and seventy-five just to keep things ahead.

"*Shel hay hiftawardesh ta pansh dileri,*" I called to Kolia.

"*Cent quatre-vingt piastres,*" Kolia translated, adding on five dollars more. "*Combien tu veux, mon ami?*" he added.

"Vingt piastres," the baker replied.

We were only five bucks in the hole from Kolia's original estimate.

"*D'accord,*" Kolia agreed. "*Te xal o rako lengo gortiano*—May the cancer eat their gullets, these greedy *Gazhe*," he said to me in Romani.

The baker and two other men helped us carry the work over to the elevator where we loaded it inside and the baker started the contraption. Then we carried everything into an enclosed area behind the factory, well sheltered from the public and the *Afrikaiya*. Kolia and I went to the station wagon, changed into our working clothes and collected the tools and equipment. We returned to the basins and I filled up the old metal bath with water from a nearby tap, connected the blowtorch to the propane cylinder, lit it, and placed the torch so that the roaring flame was against the side of the bath. Then I threw three packets of lye into the water and, when it reached boiling point, I washed the mixing bowls to remove the encrusted dough. Afterwards, I dried them off with the heat of the torch and washed them again with muriatic acid to make sure that only the metal remained. Then came the plating, Kolia's specialty. First he heated the basin until it got to the right temperature. If it was too cold, the tin wouldn't take and if it was too hot, the basin would melt. "*Kana nakadion*—When they swallow," was the only definition of this point I ever got from Kolia who seemed to know by instinct exactly when it was reached.

When the basin was ready to swallow, he would pick up one

of his tin strips which looked like large flat icicles. He made them himself by melting down old tin in a crucible and letting it run onto the sand to form these "tongues of tin" as he called them. As he applied the tin strip to the heated basin, it melted and he smeared the resulting liquid over an ever-widening area of the basin by means of a rag, all the while playing the blowtorch over the basin to keep it at the right temperature.

In the old days, he told me, the Gypsies used to heat the basins over a charcoal fire but nowadays, he confided, the blowtorch is better.

While Kolia was working on the basins I made the temper, which consisted of a pot of muriatic acid into which we dropped zinc photoplates, bummed or bought from movie theatres. The resulting mess, called *zalzairo* in Romani, smelt horrible and if used indoors it would rot every article made of cloth within yards.

As one area of the basin was plated, Kolia would move on to another. Finally, he would go over the whole basin, evening out the plated tin so that no ridges, lumps, hollows or unplated areas remained. One day, I hoped I'd be able to emulate this craft of his, but for the time being I could hardly hold an acetylene torch without endangering somebody's good looks or property.

Even Kolia had paid a price for his ability. His eyeballs were scarred from the glare of the torch and the fumes of the acid, and his hands were burned black.

Kolia continued with his plating while I heated some more water in the old bath. Then, after I checked the aluminum pots and pans to see if any of the handles had loose rivets, I went back to the station wagon to collect the *dopo*. In North America, this *dopo* is usually the axle from an old car with one wheel mount and part of the axle sawn off and the other wheel mount left on. It serves as a base while the hollow axle takes the stems of the numerous forms that are usually homemade and can be fitted snugly into the axle to form a rough and ready anvil. I inserted the proper form, took a hammer and bashed the rivets flat again. By now, the water was boiling so I added some lye, then took the *kleshto*, or metal tongs, and grabbed the pots and pans, one by one, and twirled them around in the bubbling mixture. In a few seconds they came out clean. I laid them in a row to be washed later with water to remove all traces of the lye.

By now, Kolia had completed all the plating and we washed the basins and the pots and pans with water. Kolia returned to the factory and collected a gang of men to help us bring them back inside. The manager paid us promptly. On our way out, Kolia slipped the head baker his twenty dollars. This, it seems, was part of the normal business procedure in such places. Everybody was pals and everybody took his bite.

"Listen," Kolia said as he opened the door of the car after we had got ready to leave, "listen, I forgot to tell the baker to wash the basins again before he uses them."

"But we washed them," I argued.

"I know," he agreed. "But there' s always a little water that collects in the bottom after a few hours. It has acid in it and it could be dangerous if they put the dough in right away. Somebody might get poisoned."

"So what?" I said. "They're only *Gazhe*."

He gave me a funny look. "I know. But if we poison the *Gazhe*, who would we work for?"

He had a point, I thought, as I watched him go back into the factory. When he returned, we drove to a combination restaurant-bar which was one of the social centres of the town. While we relaxed over a beer, Kolia took the money we had been paid, deducted the expenses and divided the profit equally. My share came to sixty-two dollars, almost as much as I used to make in a whole week back in the office. After dinner, we had a few more beers.

I turned on the jukebox but Kolia didn't care for the music. He preferred to talk.

"In North America," he went on, "the Gypsies are losing their own music. Now we have to come to the *Gazhe* to be entertained. In the old days, we used to travel in large bands. We lived in camps and when the men came home from a successful job we used to feast, dance and sing. Now look at us. First, the Nazis came and slaughtered us, then the Communists destroyed our old way of life forever. So we went west, to France, Italy, Spain, England and America. Here nobody kills us but our culture is dying. We hide in the cities from the *Gazhe* and at times, like today, even from one another. Soon there'll be none of us left. Wherever we go we're always outlaws."

"But you're still free, Kolia," I argued.

"Yes," he said, "like the wolf, the eagle or the fox. But there will soon be a time when we have nowhere left to go."

I said nothing and as the restaurant filled we were joined by the head baker and some of the employees of the factory and their families. French-Canadians can outdrink almost anybody but so could Kolia. I was afraid that he might spend too much money, but he was matched, round for round. Somebody arrived with an accordion, somebody else had a mouth organ and soon a violin appeared. They sang and danced old Quebec jigs and reels. Even the priest dropped in, but limited himself to a small glass of brandy.

I saw Kolia dancing with one of the girls from the factory, then they came over and joined me along with another girl. Like most of the unmarried women in these rural areas they were always on the lookout for potential husbands and I guess they had Kolia and me spotted. Personally, I certainly didn't want to get married again, but I wondered about Kolia. Most Gypsy men are married while in their teens and Kolia was well into his thirties. He never talked about women the way other Gypsy men did, with the usual jokes about sex. Whenever I picked up some sex partner, Kolia never wanted to come along. I thought it was his sense of Gypsy law. Being an older man, he might have felt that he should set an example, and promiscuity is frowned upon by the older Gypsies.

But tonight, the two girls seemed willing to go with us, no strings attached, and Kolia seemed ready to take advantage of it. We bought a case of beer and some wine and went to our room with our playmates. I was soon relaxing after my nookie but Kolia still remained sitting in the large armchair, drinking and showing no signs of making any advances towards the girl who by now was starting to get angry.

"*Est-ce que je suis laide, moi?*" she challenged Kolia.

He mumbled something.

There now followed a tirade from the girl. She insulted Kolia and threw doubts on his virility.

I was getting fed up with the whole thing. I'd had my piece and now I only wanted to sleep.

Kolia's girlfriend finally left in a huff, and mine got dressed and followed a few minutes later.

"What happened, Kolia?" I asked him. "Did you get too drunk to do anything?"

"Yes," he said. "That's what happened. I couldn't do anything."

He staggered over to his bed, got in and turned off the bedlight.

The following day Kolia's love life again came up. We had another job to do at a large restaurant in Three Rivers where Kolia had a steady contract to keep the kitchen equipment in order. We arrived there about three o'clock and went into the kitchen where Kolia spoke to the man in charge, an Italian immigrant this time, and I saw the Gypsy chameleon adjust to the situation.

"*Buon giorno,*" he greeted the manager, "Good day my friend and fellow countryman of Naples. I believe you have work for me?"

"*Si, amico,*" the man said. He led us over to some kitchen equipment, which we examined. The stove needed a good cleaning and painting, the gas range was out of order, many jets required readjustments, numerous pots and pans were without handles or had loose rivets, the doors of the ovens were coming away at their hinges, while the range canopy was full of grease and numerous bricks in the Bar-B-Q pit were smashed.

"This will take us the rest of the day and tonight," Kolia told the man. "We'll start right away with the work that we can do while your employees are still here and do the rest tonight when the kitchen is closed."

Kolia gave the manager a rough estimate and we started by repairing the pots and pans, washing them in boiling water and lye and banging the rivets flat again. Then we repaired the loose doors of the ovens. The screws holding on the hinges had become loose and these had now to be redrilled, tapped a size larger and a larger screw inserted. I did this while Kolia worked on the gas jets.

We took a break to wait for the kitchen staff to finish for the day so we could get at the stove and range canopy. Finally, the manager told us we could start and gave Kolia a set of keys telling us to lock ourselves inside while we were working in the kitchen and to lock ourselves out when we were working on the roof. The manager left and we started. First, we went up onto the roof where Kolia lowered me slowly down the chimney of the range canopy, suspended in a special harness we had for this purpose, so that I could remove all the grease and soot from the walls. He was much too heavy to get down there so it was my lot to be the chimney sweep. I scraped off the encrusted grease with a scraper then burned off the obstinate remainder with a Benzomatic blowtorch. An electric light bulb in its protective wire cage hung beside me so I could see what I was doing. When I emerged from the chimney I was covered with grease and soot which soon washed off once we got back downstairs into the restaurant. We cleaned the gas range and the stove, buffed off the caked-up grease using an electric drill to which was attached a rubber disk covered in emery paper. Then I painted the stove with black fire-resistant enamel.

"Christ," I thought, as I daubed on the paint, "is this to be my destiny, a painter of stoves and canopies?" Anyway, it paid more than historical research and model shipbuilding.

Finally, we had only the Bar-B-Q pit left to do. It was soon clean and I looked at the broken bricks.

"What'll we do now?" I asked Kolia. "We have no spare bricks with us."

He just smiled and started removing the bricks that were smashed. "Boil some water and put lye in it."

When I had the water ready he brought over about thirty bricks, all broken, and washed them with his tongs one by one in the bubbling water. Once washed, they looked like brand new bricks that had been smashed. Then he replaced them in the Bar-B-Q pit the other way round so that the broken ends were hidden to the rear of the wall. When he got through, even I would have sworn that he'd installed new ones. Now he could bill the restaurant for thirty-five new bricks at $2.50 a brick. He turned to me and grinned.

"*Gazho si dilo*—The non-Gypsy is a fool."

By six A.M. we had finished and we sat around talking and eating in the kitchen.

"Why don't you get yourself a wife?" Kolia asked as I made myself a shishkebab.

"I had one—you know that. But we broke up."

"You could buy a Gypsy girl," Kolia suggested. "I could arrange it."

I swallowed my mouthful. "Yes, you probably could," I agreed. "With you Gypsies there's no problem. You just pick out the one you want, pay her father the marriage dowry, set her up in a fortunetelling store and have a bunch of kids. With me it's not that simple. I was cursed to be educated by the *Gazhe*."

"Sometimes I wish I could read," Kolia said. "I'd give anything to be able to read a book or write a letter on a typewriter like you."

"Gypsies are better off illiterate," I said. "You can go anywhere in the world and earn your living by your own wits and skills, you have no mental hang-ups because you haven't read all the drivel written by other hung-up scribblers, you have no doubts or fears. You don't know how lucky you are. Look at me. If I wasn't your partner I'd probably starve to death. I can do the work with you but I can't get it like you. You have a way of dealing with people, some instinct. I see it working, but I haven't got it. Do you know what the sum total is of all the writings in all the books by all the geniuses, Kolia?"

"What?"

"Stupidity, Kolia, stupidity. Only the simple people like you Gypsies really make sense."

"But you're always reading."

I agreed. "That's my only hope now. To keep on reading until I know where to stand."

"Where's that?" he asked.

"With you, Kolia, and the rest of the illiterate Gypsies. I have to get where you are the long-way round."

The head cook now arrived, started the gas ranges, chased most of the cockroaches off the pans of raw potatoes and dumped them into the bubbling fat. Then the manager appeared, inspected the work and seemed satisfied. He asked Kolia the price.

"Two hundred and ninety dollars."

"*Quanto per me?*" he asked, "What's my cut?"

Kolia smiled. "Twenty dollars."

"Thirty," the man argued.

He settled for twenty-five, eventually. My share would come to about a hundred and twenty after the expenses, and they hadn't been high for this job. Considering the saving we had made on the bricks we'd come out well ahead. I made out a bill and the manager paid us right away. Kolia slipped him his *mita*, or bribe, and we got into the car and divided the profit.

We drove towards Ottawa-Hull, bypassing Montreal on the south shore. The highway ahead of us stretched into the sunset as we neared Hull. Kolia had to squint to see against it. My muscles were aching and I still had bits of grit and soot in my nose and under my fingernails. But I was happy. I relaxed, smoking. Kolia began singing an old Kalderash song.

Molatnivas soro riato,
Tehara ande diminyatsa
Makiovavas amalensa
Xasaravas muri viatsa.

I was having a wild party with friends
All through the night till dawn
I was drinking and wasting my life
So I took myself, mother, and went away
I came to two roads, one going far, one going near
I looked up and I looked down but I saw nobody
But I saw a little bird, then it was not a little bird
It was my dear little dead mother
And she was crying tears of blood
Her hair was hanging down all undone.

Before me are two roads, which should I take?
The Gypsy road or the non-Gypsy road?
I took the non-Gypsy road but I didn't go far
I got into big trouble, big trouble
I ate the leg of a goose and they threw me in jail
Then I ate the drumstick of a gander and they threw me
          in the dungeon

As we approached Hull, Kolia turned into a large shopping plaza to buy some things for his parents, a box of cigarillos for his father, two cans of anchovies and a pair of new shoes for himself. He was always buying new shoes and throwing his "old" ones away. In a few days he would have spilled *zalzairo* on this new pair. I kept telling him to keep an old pair to work in but he refused to listen.

I bought myself some decent work clothes to replace the odds and ends I'd been using to work in and we drove away. We made one more stop at the liquor commission to buy a couple of bottles of apple cider for Kolia's mother, a bottle of *rakiya* for his father and some beer for ourselves.

The old people were just finishing supper when we arrived. The old lady knew we were coming and had made enough for us. The more I lived among these Kalderash Gypsies the more I became convinced that they had some kind of telepathy that enabled them to communicate with one another, especially if they were closely related or members of the same family.

The house had been rearranged since the last time Kolia and I had been home and old Doikitsa showed me where I was supposed to sleep and what towels and dishes I was to use. You can't wash clothes, dishes and babies in the same pan and every Gypsy has his own eating utensils, towels and soap. Other dishes and utensils were set aside for guests and still others for pregnant women. Certain towels were for the face and others for the nether regions and there were different coloured soaps in the sink, each with an allowed function.

Doikitsa heated up the supper for us while Kolia and I talked with Valodia as he sipped his *rakiya*. Kolia and his father spoke in Romani and sometimes I didn't catch a certain word or expression, since their basic Romani was much mixed with words from other tongues. I took out my notebook to write down the unfamiliar terms. Some of them I could guess at, such as *lantso*—chain, from Rumanian or *pomozhnik*—helper, from Serbo-Croat.

The old man started blasting Kolia for something, and Kolia, one of the strongest men I have ever met, just sat there meekly and endured his father's tirade. The old fellow kept turning to me asking my agreement as to what he was saying and I nodded my head even though I wasn't really aware of what it was all about.

"It's time you got married, my son," Kolia's father said. "You're too old to live alone. You need a woman to make your meals, fix your clothes, bear my grandchildren. Most Roms are married before they have hair on their chests."

"I have a chosen one," Kolia said defensively. "Tinka, the daughter of Mitcho the Russian Gypsy. But he won't let me have her until I pay the dowry."

The old man stared at him. "Then steal her," he suggested. "You're my son, aren't you? Your mother's family chased us all through Serbia and well into Rumania when we eloped. But that was in the old days when Gypsies were men. Today we are half *Gazhe*, buying our wives and haggling over the price of the dowry like Arabs in the market place. What are you, a Rom, a *Gazho*, or a *pampuritsa?*"

Kolia said nothing and the atmosphere was cleared by the old lady who brought us our supper of *sarmi*, or stuffed cabbage rolls,

15

highly spiced, which I ate with difficulty. After supper we drank and smoked. The old man really enjoyed his cigarillos. With his Mexican poncho and exotic green felt hat he had the air of Pancho Villa or some other *bandido* and his fierce-looking moustache recalled days long past when Gypsy *palikaria* carried weapons against the Turks in the Balkan wars of liberation. The old lady puffed away on her pipe like a veteran, muttering at the old man and glancing periodically at me.

What the hell had I done wrong now, washed my hands with the wrong soap or something?

"What are they mumbling about?" I asked Kolia in French.

"They like you," he said. "You remind them of somebody, somewhere, a Gypsy who was killed in the war. They're trying to think of a name to call you—a Gypsy name."

"I have it now," the old lady burst out. "Yanko, we'll call you Yanko."

"Yanko," I said aloud. It did seem to fit.

— 3 —

A year passed, during which time Kolia, his parents and I returned to Montreal and set ourselves up in an old house with a store front on St. Urbain Street about a block above St. Catherine. It was summer again and I had changed. My body had become more muscular from working with Kolia and my habits and mannerisms were now so fully those of a Gypsy that I was no longer ever mistaken to be a *Gazho*.

Again Kolia and I were driving towards Ottawa, this time to look for work and for some other reason that Kolia hadn't explained to me. I was smiling as I sat beside him in the car remembering my divorce.... when Linda's mother had told the lawyers to draw up all the papers; then they couldn't find me. They'd tried the office I had worked in, the night school I'd attended, El Cortijo and the other hangouts I'd frequented. But no dice, no Ronald Lee.... It was a mere impulse that I called Linda to see if she'd ever received any mail for me at our old address after I'd split.

"People don't disappear in Canada," she told me. "Where the hell were you?"

I told her I'd been in the States for a while and left it at that. We met in El Cortijo on Clark Street. She and Larry, my replacement, belonged to a free-wheeling sort of jet-set group, both earned good money and they were confidently building themselves careers, as the ads say. She was wearing velvet slacks, a white turtleneck sweater and red shoes. Larry had a brown corduroy jacket, purple ascot, grey flannel trousers and a pair of green suede shoes. I couldn't seem to make them understand who Kolia was. They kept asking me what language we were speaking.

They paid me fifty dollars for my co-operation in the divorce. One of the hippie girls from El Cortijo, a skinny little thing who was

19

always watching me in former days, posed with me for the evidence photo in the studio of a free-lance photographer just down the street and got ten bucks for her trouble. Then our divorce bill came up, the hammer thumped and some senile, doddering old clunker of a senator scribbled his name on a piece of paper and five years of marriage, argument, hope, frustration and the occasional piece of ass ceased to have any more meaning.

We drove down a dip in the highway, climbed to the top of a low hill and I suddenly saw Ottawa ahead of us. It was about noon and the streets were busy with the luncheon crowd.

Ottawa is a strange city. You can't love it as you do Montreal, but you don't hate it as you do Toronto. Nobody lives there unless he has to and nobody goes there if he can avoid doing so. The natives, if they are thirsty or looking for commercial sex, all go to Hull, its evil French twin across the river in *La Belle Province*.

We entered the downtown area and drove into the section where the Parliament buildings are located. I noticed a Gypsy fortunetelling joint right across the road opposite where our Government sits. How appropriate, I thought, a sort of balance.

A short, thickset man of about fifty was standing in front of the Gypsy store wearing a black tropical suit, flashy purple shirt, white panama hat, green shoes and numerous gold rings. He seemed an American-born Gypsy by the look of him.

"Who is that?" I asked Kolia.

"Mitcho, the son of Boyo and the father of Tinka the girl I want to marry," he explained. "I don't want him to see me."

Kolia turned up a side street, stopped the car and lit a cigarette.

"Yanko," he sounded as if he were about to entrust a great mission. "Yanko, I want you to do something very important for me."

"What, blow up the Parliament buildings?"

He smiled. "I want you to go into that store and act like a customer. Talk to Tinka if you can. She has a ring with a blue stone on the second finger of her left hand. Make sure you're alone with her and show her this."

He took off his own gold ring, his totem, the head of a wolf was worked into the design of the Ruveshti, his mother's clan.

"Tell her I want to meet her somewhere to talk, alone," Kolia went on. "They're suspicious that Tinka and I might try to elope. They don't know you. You might be able to pass as a *Gazho* customer."

I did not share his confidence about my passing as a *Gazho*, but I got out and walked around to the store. The guy outside had vanished and the front part of the *ofisa*, where the women told fortunes, was deserted. This front part was separated from the living quarters in the rear by a thick, heavy curtain. It was decorated with tapestries, copper plates, buddhas and crucifixes to impress the clientele. I noticed the licence hanging on the wall and felt as if I were being watched. A young Gypsy woman came out from behind the drapes and studied me.

Gypsies usually cater to the style of the particular customer; for the old man, there is the vigorous matron with the hefty backside and magnificent bust; for the middle-aged lady, there is the wise old matriarch; for the young man, like me, if he seems respectable and polite, the young, voluptuous Gypsy temptress; or if he is rough and uncouth-looking, the hard-fisted, loud-mouthed Gypsy Amazon who can lay him out on the carpet, minus his teeth, if he puts his hand in the wrong place. Again, if there is no Amazon available to deal with him, a sweet young Gypsy madonna will suddenly appear and breastfeed her baby as she tells his fortune. Every man from truck driver to Member of Parliament has that ingrained respect for motherhood that prevents him from trying to get a cheap feel.

The bells jingled as the curtains fell back into place and the woman came towards me. A typical North-American Gypsy, she was dark-skinned with long black hair tied in a pony tail with a big yellow butterfly bow just over her nape. She was wearing the colourful ankle-length Gypsy dress, golden slippers and a low-cut blouse. She was short and plump and approached me with a masterful, matriarchal air. I saw the ring, but with a red stone. Tinka must have changed her politics with the government across the street.

"You want a reading, mister?" she asked in a heavy, throaty voice.

"Yes, please," I smiled pleasantly. "I have a love problem."

She used the polite approach. "Sit down," she told me, motioning towards the special chair that Gypsies keep in their homes for non-Gypsies to sit on. No Gypsy ever sits on it so I chose the sofa nearby. She frowned, but said nothing, as she got a small footstool and sat down on it right in front of me, giving me a splendid view of her tits. Then she started the usual spiel. I let her go on for a while as she examined my hand, spotting the stains of the special acid that all Coppersmith Gypsies get on their skin.

I showed her Kolia's ring and by the way she looked at it I knew this was Tinka.

"*Rom sim*," I whispered. "I'm a Gypsy, Kolia's partner. He wants to see you tonight to talk."

She thought for a moment, reached into the *kisi*, or purse, sewn into her Gypsy skirt, undid the strings and handed me a book of penny matches with the advertising and address of a bar on it.

"Here," she told me, "at ten tonight."

"Good," I replied, "Kolia will be happy."

"Don't talk any more," she went on as she grabbed my mitt and assumed a professional attitude, just as an elderly woman, obviously her mother, came into the parlour from behind the curtains and smiled benevolently at me. She was the biggest woman I've ever seen in my life and I now knew why Kolia always referred to her as the *Brashka*, or female frog. She was a huge misshapen lump with hardly any hair. God, I thought in horror, is this what Tinka will look like some day? There is a saying among the Gypsies. "*Chi perel e pabai dur katar o kasht*—The apple never falls far from the tree."

Tinka finished reading my palm, told me I was going to meet a woman and get married very shortly and asked me for five dollars. I made a mental note to ask Kolia for it. Once a Gypsy woman gets her hands on money, often death cannot reclaim it.

I left the store, walked up the street, entered the restaurant, strolled through the kitchen and into the back yard where I climbed over a low wall, ignoring the shouts of protest from the kitchen staff. I found myself in a narrow lane from where I took an equally devious route back to Kolia.

If anybody had followed me from the store they'd have a hell of a long wait before I came back out of the restaurant.

Kolia was glad to see me. I gave him the matchbook and told him what time she wanted to meet him. He suggested we have a drink, after which we went to a succession of rooming houses until we found one that suited Kolia. He settled for a large, expensive room with two beds and nice furnishings. I guess he was planning to elope with Tinka in desperation. If he came home again without a wife, his father would probably disown him. He paid the landlady, a middle-aged French Canadian woman and explained that he was

French, a refugee from those terrible Arabs in Morocco. I had to be Spanish, his apprentice.

"We're plumbers," he added. I smiled. Plumbing is a trade forbidden to Gypsies by their own law. A Gypsy man would be defiled by handling toilet fixtures and would run the grave risk of being socially ostracized. Gypsies don't even sit on a toilet seat but sort of squat over it. We left the rooming house and went to a restaurant to wait out the time. At nine-thirty, Kolia couldn't wait any longer and we left together.

"*Si tut love,* Yanko?" he asked me, as we stood in the street outside.

"Enough money for what I'll need. I'm not going on a date."

"See you later." He got into the car and drove off.

I felt a certain excitement in the air as I walked along the street. It was a humid night and the air seemed tinged with electricity. There was also a full moon—a dangerous time, I thought, remembering that old Gypsies feared the moon. Girls gave me come-on stares as they passed me on the street and I began to realize that Ottawa does have some advantages. I've never seen so many sexy women on the make as in Ottawa; there seems to be always a shortage of men in the city.

A few drops of rain fell and thunder rumbled in the distance. Looking for a place of refuge, I saw a stairway, red carpet and all, leading up to a bar. The top of the stairs gave into a large dimly lit nightclub. Christ, I thought, this couldn't be Ottawa. Kolia must have crossed over into Hull while I was daydreaming. At the far end of the lounge there was a small stage, then three long rows of tables leading to the long bar at the end. A few women were sitting on bar stools under the T.V., some obviously small-time hoods and fringe underworld characters had occupied a table, and there was a large group of teenagers clustered at the tables near the stage. I walked down between the rows and took a seat at an unoccupied table, ordered a beer and wished that Kolia, or Alec, or somebody was with me to make something happen. Alone, I never seemed to get into any interesting situations. The place gradually filled up as I drank my required quota of beers and listened to the music of the jukebox. Then, about ten-thirty, two girls came into the bar. They looked like office girls and as they came closer to my table looking for somewhere to sit down I recognized one of them and made a sign for her to come over. At first she seemed suspicious, then, recognizing me, she walked over. Her friend followed.

"Marie," I said. "Where've you been all these years?"

She sat down. "Mind if my friend joins the table?"

"That's O.K.," I said.

"I've been moving around quite a bit since my husband left me," Marie said. "I just came from Toronto. This is Edith," she pointed to her friend. "What have you been doing?"

"Same thing as you, after my wife left me."

"She left you?" Marie said. "I can't believe it."

"Well, she did, chronologically," I explained. "She walked out on me, so I left and then she came back and took over the apartment. Larry's living there now."

"You mean that salesman guy."

"That's the one."

We talked for a while, discussing old friends and the places we'd been to. Edith got bored and drifted off to join some guys at a nearby table. I asked Marie to dance. The stage was crowded and we had to dance close.

"What you doing now?" she asked me. "You got anybody lined up?"

I shook my head. "You?"

"Nope," she said, "it's pretty hard to meet anybody decent nowadays, especially in the city."

"How do you know I'm decent?" I asked.

She smiled. "I know you from way back, but we were both married then, remember."

The music stopped and we stood there on the stage.

"Would it have made any difference if we hadn't been?" I asked, kidding her along.

"Let's sit down," she suggested.

I ordered two drinks and she left to go to the washroom. I studied her as she walked away, her long, waist-length black hair, petite figure. Now she was available. Was I?

She came back, sat down and put her head on my shoulder. I stroked her hair.

"I'm glad I met you again," she told me. "We're both looking for something, just a couple of drifters floating around with nowhere to go."

I kissed her. "I'd like to see more of you, but tomorrow I'll be leaving. If I get back in a month or so, where will you be?"

"Why do you travel so much?" she asked. "You got itchy feet or something."

"I'm a Gypsy. That's something you don't know about me."

She didn't really understand but took it like a typical Canadian, thinking I meant a person who travels a lot like a salesman, folksinger, or prostitute.

"Have you gone beat?" she asked.

"What's the difference?" I philosophized. "Gypsies, beatniks, we're all outcasts."

"You're funny," she sighed, putting her head back on my shoulder.

Edith returned to the table, obviously stoned out of her mind, along with two of the guys she had been sitting with. One of them had picked her up and now it seems the other was planning to move in on us. He pulled up a chair beside Marie and started playing with her hair. I had moved away out of politeness when they sat down.

"Come on, honey, be sociable," he said to Marie. "Be a good squaw and I'll buy you all the booze you can drink. Just be nice to me baby, you won't be sorry."

Marie reached down and pulled up her knee-length skirt. I saw her stocking tops for an instant, then the knife glittered in the flickering light about three inches away from the guy's Adam's apple.

"Let go of my hair, you rotten white sonovabitch," Marie told him.

"You ready to leave?" I asked her.

We headed for the door, followed by the drunk. His friend stayed at the table with Edith. At least the odds were even. We reached the top of the stairs as the punk closed in. Marie offered me the knife, but I pushed her hand away just as the romeo lunged for me. My right hand closed firmly around his testicles, then gripped tightly as my shoulder fitted naturally into his stomach. In a few seconds he was on his way downstairs landing with a thud at the bottom.

"Let's go," I said to Marie as I saw the bouncers and waiters moving toward us. I grabbed her hand and we ran downstairs, skirting her attacker who was now getting groggily to his knees.

"*Ostiskwah*," Marie yelled and clobbered him with her heavy handbag. He went back to sleep.

Once outside we ran for a while, then grabbed a taxi. I told Marie to give him her address.

"Go there first," I told him, "then you can take me home later."

We didn't say much on the way to her place. I held her hand and stroked her hair; she was trembling now that the excitement was over. The cab finally stopped, I got out and turned to help Marie. She didn't move.

"Will I see you again if I go home tonight?"

"Who knows?" I told her.

She looked at me and seemed to be trying to make up her mind.

"I'm no pig," she said.

"Did I say you were?" I replied.

She fumbled in her handbag for a few seconds as the hackie sat back and lit a cigarette. Then she got out, kissed me and slipped a key into my hand.

"No strings attached?" I asked.

She shook her head.

"O.K.," I told her. "We'll go to my place tonight and pick up your gear tomorrow." She got back in the cab and I followed.

As the driver started up I thought, "Poor Kolia, is he ever in for a shock!"

O Del, or God, is the card of the universal intellect. According to the Romani folk religion, God, or *godi* in Romani from the Sanskrit *goda* (brain, intellect, etc.), is a universal force that animates all living beings. This force in itself is neither good nor evil, it is the use to which the force is put that causes good or evil to occur. Here we see the true picture, in the left hand the figure holds the symbol of death, in his right the flower of life (lotus) while the poppy of illusion is held by the third hand which is explained by the *trushula* or trident on the forehead of the figure. The centre prong is the application of the intellect in the hands of the Gypsy, the left prong the symbol of application for evil, the right prong, the application for good. The Gypsy attitude is to be found, again in the tarot cards, in the picture of a snake wrapping itself around a knife. The knife is the Gypsy, the snake is his enemy. In attempting to crush the knife the snake itself is destroyed. This is how the Gypsy employs the universal intellect, as the major weapon in his struggle against those would destroy him.

This is what Yanko learns from Kolia.

29

— 4 —

Marie had fallen asleep and I was drowsing off watching the moon-light filtering into the room through the Venetian blinds. The alarm clock on the table nearby said two-thirty and Kolia hadn't come back yet. The storm hadn't arrived either, but thunder still rumbled in the distance.

I heard whispered sounds in the hallway, somebody turned a key in the lock and the door opened with hinges squeaking. A female voice giggled softly. A deep male voice told her, in Romani, to be quiet.

I pretended to be asleep and covered Marie so that they couldn't see her in the dim light. Kolia and Tinka started to undress, their backs to each other as dictated by Gypsy law. Tinka got into bed first. I got a view of her brown rump as she climbed onto the white sheets and pulled them over her. Kolia slipped out of his clothes. Getting in beside her, he stubbed his toe on the iron leg of the bedpost and let out with a loud "*carrajo*".

There now followed sounds of heavy breathing, giggling, whis-pered endearments, then, loud kissing noises and finally the sounds of violent wrestling and wild thrashing.

"What a racket," I thought. Kolia makes love like he was repairing a steam jacket cauldron. Tinka had been married before and she got straight down to business. Soon all was quiet again.

"Are you awake, Yanko?" Kolia said in a loud whisper.

"How could I sleep with all that noise going on?"

He got up, put his shoes on and turned on the small bedlamp then smiled at me. He stood there naked except for his shoes, socks and the crucifix around his neck.

"I'm eloping. Look."

He raised the blanket slightly to show the back of a woman's

31

head, raven black hair in a long pony tail tied with the crushed remnants of a yellow butterfly bow.

"That's Tinka," he said proudly.

"That's nice," I told him. "Come here. I have something to show you."

He came over, his eyes squinting. He was really getting nearsighted. I lifted the bedclothes to show him the back of Marie's head. She was still asleep. He saw the long hair, the wilted red rose over her ear, the yellowish skin, and mistook her for a Gypsy girl.

"*Arak tu bre*," I warned him as he moved closer. He had almost stepped on Marie's panties which were lying on the floor. He sprang aside like a soldier who just heard the shout of "Mine!" his eyes searching desperately for other pieces of taboo female underwear.

"Who's daughter is she?" he asked.

"A good girl," I told him.

He stared incredulous as Marie suddenly sat up in bed, half awake and confused, her long hair in disarray. She saw Kolia standing there naked, turned away and pulled the blankets up to hide her breasts.

"Where did you find her?" Kolia asked. "Is she one of the Stevenson girls?"

"She's not a Gypsy, Kolia," I told him. "She's a Canadian Indian."

Marie turned to him again. Kolia sprang over to the couch, covered his nudity with his shirt and then slipped into his trousers.

"Get dressed, everybody," he ordered suddenly. "We have to leave right away before Tinka's father misses her and starts a search."

Kolia and I got dressed first, then sat with our backs to the women as they started dressing in the moonlight. Tinka finally spoke in Romani.

"Who the hell is the girl with your partner, Kolia. A *kurva*?"

She pointed at Marie who was sitting on the edge of the bed clutching her handbag. Marie was confused by our use of Romani and looked at Tinka, perhaps for feminine solidarity, but her eyes soon quailed before the penetrating stare of the feline Gypsy huntress. Kolia struggled as best he could to explain to Tinka who Marie was.

"They love each other," he said trying to make the situation acceptable to her. "They want to get married. *Iwon nashentar—* They're eloping too."

Tinka went over to Marie and put her arm around her shoulders. "That's nice," she said. "Now I won't be alone anymore."

Tinka, with her matriarchal Gypsy instinct, was already preparing my poor Marie to be a sort of lady-in-waiting, hair comber, errand runner and general domestic. This often happens to a non-Gypsy girl who marries into a Gypsy *kumpaniya*.

"Who are these people?" Marie asked me. "What's going on here?"

"They're Gypsies like me," I explained. "This man, Kolia, is my partner and Tinka there is his wife-to-be. He's stealing her and her father is after them."

"Gypsies... Eloping," she seemed scared. "Christ, Ron, when you told me you were a Gypsy I didn't think you meant this."

"Nobody ever does," I replied.

She gave Kolia a frightened glance. Kolia, one of the friendliest and most peaceful of men I've ever met always seemed to give everyone the idea that he was some kind of murderous cutthroat. I went over to Marie and put my arm around her, kissed her and stroked her hair. Gypsies frown on displays of affection in public but this kid was scared.

"We have to leave," I told her. "Are you coming with us?"

She looked at me and nodded. "Can we go to my place first and pick up my stuff?"

We started packing our things as Marie went out to find the washroom. She soon rushed back in, pursued by the irate landlady.

"Gentlemen," the battle-ax told us. "I assumed that you were decent catholic men of honour. We don't allow women like this in here at night. This is a respectable house."

She looked again at Marie and the ingrained fear of French-Canadians for Indians took over. "*Mon Dieu, une sauvagesse,*" she gasped.

"What's that old bag yelling about?" Tinka asked, as she stood there defiantly in her full Gypsy costume, her hands arrogantly on her hips.

"*Une gitane aussi,*" the landlady exploded. "*Messieurs,* get these whores out of here immediately before I call the police."

Kolia slipped her a ten dollar bill which had the immediate effect of restoring tranquillity. We all left the rooming house and piled into the station wagon. Marie could take her leak later.

We drove through Ottawa and over the bridge to the house in the Hull slum where Marie was staying. The lights were still on. Kolia and Tinka stayed in the car as Marie and I walked up the stairs. She pushed the door; it wasn't locked. We went inside and found a small group of Indians enjoying the last phase of a party. She was living with an older Indian couple, who rented rooms to young Indian drifters like her. There was always a string of new arrivals to replace those who moved on in an endless search to find that white brotherhood they been told about back in the mission schools. One guy was strumming a guitar softly; another was lying on the couch eating roast chicken; an older man and his wife were sitting at the table. At first they gave me hostile glances until Marie explained who I was and what I was doing there. Then they became friendly and her landlady asked us to sit down and have some food. They had the same hospitality as the Gypsies.

I went with Marie to her room where she collected her belongings. She didn't have much, a few clothes, a couple of books, some cheap jewelry, her bible, and her rosary. It all fitted nicely into one small suitcase. She explained to her landlady that she was leaving with me. The landlady gave us a parcel of food to eat on the way. Her husband shook hands with me.

"You take good care of that girl, you hear," he said, "and drop in and see us next time you're passing through."

We went back to the car, Kolia was sitting in the front with Tinka, and Marie and I had to get in the back with the luggage, tools and other junk. The Indian couple stood in the doorway and waved to us as Kolia drove away. There was something genuinely sad about these city Indians. First, they had been pushed into reservations where there was nothing but cold, hunger and unemployment. Then they'd come hopefully to the white man's cities, only to be driven into the slum ghettos.

The gypsies were different. If they'd ever had a land of their own it had been swiped so long ago that it had long since ceased to have any valid meaning.

The sun finally rose, and with it, came the torrential downpour I had anticipated. The rain lashing the countryside seemed somehow symbolic of this harsh, ruggedly beautiful land.

Our visibility was soon cut off. The windshield wipers were useless, but the old station wagon lurched onwards, seemingly immune to the elements.

"Where are we going?" I called to Kolia.

"Toronto," came his reply.

"Good God, man," I moaned. "That's almost two hundred miles."

Marie and I were really uncomfortable by now. We tried to fit ourselves somehow among the luggage, the gas gun, propane tank, boxes of rags, Tinka's feather-filled *plapono* and the old metal bath. I found a bottle of brandy that Kolia kept for medicinal purposes and Marie and Tinka helped me finish it off. Soon the three of us were half-stoned and relaxed, immune to the storm outside. Kolia was drunk on love. He kept turning and smiling at Tinka. Marie finally fell asleep and I stretched her gently on the rear seat while I drowsed off as best I could on top of the pile of suitcases. I woke up some hours later and found myself crumpled on the floor, my head resting on the propane gas cylinder and the blowtorch under my spine. A ringing headache told me that I hadn't slept too well, but at least the rain had stopped and brilliant sunshine replaced the storm. Tinka was asleep and her head kept banging against the back of the front seat whenever the car hit one of the numerous potholes in the road. Kolia looked haggard, his eyes almost ready to close. Marie was still sleeping peacefully.

"Kolia, for God's sake let's stop and rest and get something to eat; then I'll drive for a while."

We stopped at a drive-in motel, which seemed almost deserted. The girl at the counter stared at us speechless. She hadn't been conditioned to face four such bedraggled specimens of humanity as now suddenly confronted her! Kolia, swarthy and half awake with his crumpled suit, wilted fedora and muddy shoes; Tinka wearing her traditional Gypsy dress and blouse and covered with barbaric jewelry; Marie with one stocking down around her ankle, braided hair and Indian headband; me wearing an old pair of denim trousers, black turtleneck sweater, an old smoking jacket and a green felt cap on top of my long hair, and three days' growth of whiskers.

We chose a table, ordered a meal and relaxed. Tinka seemed to be having some misgivings about her elopement. Marie was eating as mechanically as if her mind too were on something else. Kolia's face was unfathomable as he sipped his glass of milk. He really enjoyed a good glass of milk.

"Kolia," I told him. "You shouldn't drink so much milk. It's bad for you."

"Bad?" he asked. "How?"

I told him about Strontium 90, how atomic fallout got into the soil, into the grass, into the cows, and finally into his milk from where it would get into him, into his bones, and destroy him.

"It's in the milk," I explained. "In that glass you're drinking."

He held up his glass to the light, examining it.

"*Chi dikav kanchi,*" he said seriously. "I don't see anything."

"What will we do in Toronto?" I asked. "Nobody ever does much there."

He shrugged his shoulders. "Get married if we can."

We got back in the car and this time I drove, while Marie sat proudly beside me and Kolia and Tinka had to cram themselves into the back. She ripped her silk Gypsy dress on the trigger of the blowtorch and swore in Romani.

Finally we reached Toronto. I cruised around the area where I figured the Gypsies must live and spotted a short, almost midget-sized, individual. He had a devilish face, a shock of jet black hair and wore a business suit and a cloth felt cap. He walked with a jaunty swagger, his eyes darting around him. I turned to Kolia.

"He looks like a Gypsy," I said. "Maybe he'll be able to tell you of some patriarch here in the city who can perform your marriage."

I cruised alongside the strolling figure.

"Sar mai san, Roma," I called out.

He stopped, suspicion clouding his face.

"Vat you vant?" he asked in a thick, heavy Hungarian accent. He looked about ready to take off to safety up the nearest alleyway. That's what Toronto does to immigrants from anywhere but England.

"*Kon san tu?*—Who are you, what clan? Are you a Rom or a Hungarian *prosto?*"

"*Nem prosto Ungaro,*" he yelled back. "I'm a Hungarian Gypsy."

He spoke with a loud clear accent, pronouncing his Romani like Hungarian. I remembered that Kolia's father had told me that these Hungarian Gypsies had their own particular dialect of the language and that many of the younger generation spoke Romani mixed with Hungarian instead of pure Romani.

"Vat people you are?" he asked.

"Kalderash Gypsies," Kolia yelled at him, getting annoyed. "Get in the car." He got in next to Marie. His name was Jilko Yaroka.

"I play violin." he started off again. "I good *lavutash* but no more money. Nobody is vant Tsigan music."

"So what do you do for a living?" I asked him.

He grinned wickedly and gave me a sly look. "*Chorav*—I steal. Vat else you can do in Toronto?"

He had a point.

Conversation was difficult but we managed to make ourselves understood. Jilko knew a large rooming house inhabited mainly by Hungarians and Hungarian Gypsies, ex-freedom fighters, now small time crooks and petty racketeers. He told us that his uncle was the respected elder and leader of the group.

"Him give you da vedink," he told Kolia.

"Dis da place," he added, pointing to an old house just off Bloor Street. We went inside and Jilko led us along a corridor lined with shabby, once-white doors. I could smell exotic foods being cooked and could hear a babble of voices in Hungarian and Hungarian Gypsy. We reached number 23 and Jilko booted the door open to reveal a large, double room with worn linoleum, two beds with dirty mattresses, a large table and some chairs. There was also a small kitchen at the far end. Jilko left and returned a few minutes later with a fat, elderly, sad-looking man. There followed a conversation between Jilko and Kolia, which Jilko translated into Hungarian for the landlord. They finally haggled out a suitable rent, Kolia paid and the landlord left with Jilko. Our women got busy and washed the floor, rearranged the furniture and placed our bedding on the beds. Tinka rigged up a drape from some material she had brought, which now divided the large room into two smaller rooms. She and Kolia took the far end near the door, while Marie and I took the other end with the large window facing out onto the street. I saw Kolia place a large pipe wrench under his bed. He gave me a wry smile.

"In case somebody gets in," he said.

A heavy pounding on the door gave justification to Kolia's suspicions, but it was only Jilko returning with his uncle, the patriarch. The old man addressed Kolia in pure Romani.

"How are you, Gypsy gentlemen. I am Shandor, the son of Stanko."

"Come in, uncle, and sit down," Kolia invited.

The old man sat down and Kolia and I joined him. He held the staff of a patriarch in his right hand and was well dressed in a new suit with an embroidered Hungarian vest underneath. His lined and weather-beaten face told of his former life on the Hungarian plains. This was no modern North American Gypsy kingpin, but and old man who looked as if he remembered the days before the two world wars when his people had roamed the plains and forests of Hungary, Carpathia, and Moldavia.

Tinka appeared and greeted the old man.

"So you want to get married." The old man said it rather than asked it.

"Yes, uncle," Kolia told him. "I thought that you might perform the ceremony."

He studied Kolia.

"Who was your father?" he asked.

Kolia told him.

"Yes, I remember him," Shandor said. "He came to the great feast where king Yanosh was made king of the Gypsies by Marshall Pilsudski in 1937, in the big army stadium near Warsaw. All the Roma were there. But they killed him, the Germans, at Auschwitz. I still remember the promise, too, that Mussolini would give the Gypsy people a state of their own on the borders of Ethiopia. But the Nazis came and slaughtered our people. Then the Communists." His eyes became misty. "I lost all my family in the war, except for little Jilko here. He brought me to Canada. He's a good boy."

"You give big party?" Jilko asked Kolia.

The old man looked at his nephew. "Yes, Jilko," he said wistfully. "There will be a big party. All you young men can get drunk and go to the she-wolves afterwards. That's all you've got left now. *Oy Devla, Hitlerina, so kerdyan amenga.*"

"How much should I provide for the wedding?" Kolia asked.

"Nothing," the old man replied. "It will be an honour for me to help the son of my old friend, O Valodia le Yankosko. Jilko will show you where the wedding will be held. Your bride will stay with me; my own wife is not much older than her and she will prepare her for the wedding."

Kolia told Tinka to accompany the old man.

"What about her?" Tinka asked, pointing at Marie who was sitting on the bed combing her hair.

"She'll stay with us," I told Tinka. I suddenly got a mental picture of Marie living with a family of Hungarian Gypsies and trying to ask her way to the washroom.

The old man left with Tinka and Jilko and now Kolia decided that he needed some new clothes for the wedding.

"Today?" I asked him, " on Sunday?"

"I'll find some somewhere," he said and left.

I went to Marie who had disappeared behind the curtains into our section of the room. She was standing in front of the mirror wearing a Gypsy costume.

"Tinka loaned me this," she informed me. "She told me to wear it at the wedding tomorrow so that the Gypsy men won't bother me when they get drunk."

She saw the funny look on my face.

"Do I look that strange?" she asked.

"Like something from a comic opera," I said. "It takes more than a costume to make a Gypsy. But you'll learn my little Indian Carmen."

"And you'd better start teaching me that language," she went on. "If I'm going to live with you bunch of nuts I might as well learn how to talk to you." I opened my suitcase and took out a new notebook. I then wrote down the Romani alphabet I had devised and explained the approximate English values. There was only one difficult sound, a guttural x, pronounced like the Spanish *jota* but she had the sound in her own Mohawk dialect.

I wrote down a sentence and asked her to pronounce it.

"*Me voliv tu,*" she read. "What does it mean?"

"I love you," I replied, grabbing her and biting her arm.

"Damnit," she moaned. "There goes my lesson."

She grappled with me and we rolled on the floor, hugging and kissing each other. What the hell of a way to give a language course, I thought. All my years of studying were finally beginning to pay off.

I opened my eyes to Monday, the day of Kolia's wedding. Marie's hair was blocking my eyes and nose. I lifted her head, rolled over on the mattress and gave her a good slap on the backside to wake her up. I told her to get dressed before Kolia came blundering into our part of the room. I could hear him singing loudly on the other side of the curtains accompanied by the sound of water running into the wash basin. Kolia, the impatient, he must have risen early. I saw Marie, now wearing her underwear, picking up her Gypsy gown from the floor where I'd thrown it last night just before our love-making. I got up, dressed and set up sketching equipment. I was working on a sketch of Kolia.

Marie came over and looked at it.

"Where are we going when we leave her?" she asked.

"Back to Montreal," I told her, "but we'll take a place of our own, near Kolia and his wife, but not with them. When Kolia and I go away on jobs you can visit Tinka so you won't be alone. What do you think of her, anyways?"

"She's O.K., I guess," Marie told me, "for him. But she looks like she could be real mean."

"You don't miss much, do you?" I said. "Anyway, Kolia should know what he's doing. Gypsies don't think like other people when they look for a wife. If she's respectable, a good fortuneteller and follows the laws and customs, that's all they ask."

Kolia's loud voice suddenly broke out again in an old Kalderash melody.

> "*Shukar si krianga peske pateriansa*
> *Mai shukar si romni peske shavensa. . .*"

41

I translated for Marie.

"A tree is beautiful with its leaves
But a woman is more beautiful with her children
The leaves die and fall off
The children grow up and leave
But the beauty lives forever
As long as there are trees and women
Life is eternal, beauty never dies."

"What a lovely song," she said. "Will you still love me when I have a bunch of your kids running after me?"

"I'll love you until you're ninety." I made a mark on her face with my charcoal crayon. She slapped my hand playfully, then studied the sketch again.

"You think a lot of Kolia, don't you?" she said.

"I do," I replied. "I always thought that if the atomic bombs ever do come I'd like to be with him in the old car coming home from a successful job in the country, singing and enjoying a good smoke just as the sun is setting. But it'll probably happen when I'm in the toilet. That's the way Alec wanted it. 'If they won't let you live respectably, they might as well kill you with your pants down,' he used to say."

"Who's Alec?"

"Another friend of mine," I told her. "Beatnik, journalist, clown—he's somewhere in Europe now."

She admired my sketch, now almost finished.

"It's good," she told me.

"Not really," I said. "My art is something very different—I'll show you."

I got my briefcase from under the bed, opened it, took out a brown envelope, selected a colour photograph and handed it to her. It was the model of a sixteenth century galleon with its painted sails, two rows of brass cannon, four butterfly turrets and the gay streamers and pennants flying from the yardarms and the fighting tops. The triangular and lozenge designs of the Tudor shipwrights ran along the panels of the forecastle and aftercastles and the standard of Queen Elizabeth flew from the main masthead and from the flagstaff next to the gilded lantern at the end of the poop.

"It's a model of the *Ark Royal*," I explained elaborately, "flagship of the English fleet that dispersed the Spanish Armada in 1588. It's probably the most accurate model of it in the world. Nobody knows exactly what it looked like but that model is based on all the details that have come down to us of ships of that era, plus details of that particular ship as described by Hakluyt and his contemporaries, as well as details taken from textbooks by modern authorities. It took me years to get all the required data for that model."

"Gee, you must have made a fortune with these things," she said.

"Yeah," I told her. "Department stores offer me five to ten bucks each for them in quantity. They only take about six months to make, once you've done all the research and collected the data, maybe drawn your own plans as well. All that might take a year or so. So it would work out to about $1/16^{th}$ of a cent per hour at their prices. All they see is a pretty little boat that somebody whittled out on a Saturday night or a toy for some kid to play with or sail in the bathtub. I'm in the wrong country for this. It's a European art."

"Are you dressed?" Kolia yelled from the other side of the drapes.

Marie closed my sketch pad quickly. I didn't want him to see it until it was finished.

"Yes," I told him. "You can come in." I put the ship photograph back in the envelope and replaced the briefcase under the bed.

An apparition was in front of us. I burst out laughing and Marie hid her face in her hands. Kolia was wearing a black tuxedo, starched white shirt, black bow tie, white carnation in his buttonhole, a pair of white spats, new black shoes, and a glittering array of rings, cufflinks, tie pin and gold teeth.

His hair had been cropped so short, only a few strands stuck up on the crown.

"Kolia," I said, "what happened?"

"I got a haircut for the wedding," he said simply.

"Never mind," I lied to cheer him up. "Tinka will be proud of you. You look very elegant. It's just the sudden shock. We weren't expecting it."

Marie managed to stop laughing, she sat quietly on the floor trying not to look at Kolia, but her impish face was still ready to break out again. Then there were a series of loud thuds on the door. It was Jilko with an older man, about forty. His toothless smile, the violin under his arm, and his swarthy face told me that he was a Hungarian Gypsy musician.

"Dis Zoltan," Jilko explained. "Him play musik for da vedink."

The Gypsy wedding, like much else in our culture, is the opposite of the non-Gypsy wedding. With us, the groom is supposed to arrive first. Kolia, nervous and blushing, somehow looked more like a bride.

We all left to go to the car, but Jilko hung back. He had something to say to me privately.

"Yanko?" he asked me, his face twisted into a leer. "Yanko, you love this *Gadji* girl. She not Gypsy woman."

"Yes," I told him. "She's my future wife. And tell the rest of the *karalo* Hungarian Gypsy boys to leave her alone. She has a sharp *churi* under her dress and knows how to use it."

"O.K., Yanko," he smiled. "Is nobody bother your woman."

We all managed to squeeze into Zoltan's sportscar and we soon arrived at the rented hall which was already packed with Gypsies, mainly from Hungary. None of Tinka's people had showed up. It might be better for them if they didn't, since I noticed a couple of burly Magyars standing at the door checking on the guests as they came in. The walls were lined with long tables now covered with hams, chickens, a couple of lambs, bread, bottles of beer, wine and hard stuff. There was a large stage along the wall, opposite the door and a group of Gypsy musicians were already playing those plaintive Magyar melodies erroneously called "Gypsy music" by non-Gypsies.

The guests were sitting at the tables, eating, drinking and talking, waiting for the marriage ceremony to begin. The old patriarch had reserved a place for us at the main table. He saw us enter the hall, got up and went over to the stage where he said something to a tough-looking *tsimbalom* player. All noise ceased as the band started to play a wedding dance. Kolia didn't know the steps, his people didn't dance these Hungarian dances, but soon a milling crowd had formed and pulled him into it. The rest of us fought our way through to the table and sat down. Kolia joined us later, minus his carnation and one of his spats. Then Tinka appeared along with a group of women. The old man called for silence. Beside him was a small table with two plates containing salt and bread along with a bottle of wine. The marriage ceremony was about to begin. Kolia joined the old man and stood beside him as Tinka and her women friends joined them. The patriarch gave Kolia and Tinka bread and salt.

"May you be unto each other as salt and bread," he said in Romani. Then they drank some wine from the same glass and the old man threw the glass against the wall smashing it into fragments.

"*Baxt, sastimus,*" the crowd roared, "*Édes éljen!*"

Hungarian and Romani toasts were shouted. The music started up again compelling the guests to dance. Many surged toward the bridal couple. I put my arm protectively around Marie as some gigantic garlic-smelling Gypsy loomed over her, trying to shake Kolia's hand. I found a glass and took a shot of whisky, yelling at Kolia.

"*Baxt, sastimus, wortakona. Te del o Del tuke but shave.* Luck and health, partner. May God grant you many children."

Kolia and Tinka finally broke free of the well-wishers and made their way to the table. Tinka didn't sit with him but further down and still with her women escort. Kolia shared the bottle of wine with the bridal party, then broke the bottle as the gaiety continued and the music played without stopping. As one musician grew tired, another replaced him. A Gypsy woman now led a crowd of women and girls around the hall as she brandished a nondescript flag from the end of a long pole. Tinka had been married before and this must have been either a sign of courtesy or ignorance on the part of the women. It symbolized that Tinka was a virgin, since the flag was a symbolic bedsheet stained with her blood after the bridal night. A bit later, another woman passed around with a loaf of bread that had been hollowed out. The guests placed money inside and were given a silk head scarf in return. The money would be given later to Kolia and Tinka as a wedding present.

Now Kolia went through the ceremony of kidnapping the bride. A group of Hungarian Gypsies surrounded Tinka, while Kolia, Jilko, Zoltan and some other Gypsies including me ceremonially attacked them to gain possession of the bride. In the old days, Kolia had told me, the kinsmen of the bride would defend her fiercely and there were often bloody scuffles. Nowadays, it had become more symbolic and was all in good fun, although a couple of tipsy Gypsies had to be forcibly separated.

We finally captured Tinka, and Kolia led her out of the hall in spite of her loud "protests." The party continued and I rejoined

Marie. As the Hungarian Gypsies drank more, they became more melancholy and instead of the fast dances and gay singing, they began wailing plaintive dirges in Romani and Hungarian. One old matriarch got onto the stage and there was silence as everybody listened to her song.

> "*Oy marde ma, Mamo, hay shude ma ando baro shantso le mulensa.*
>
> Oh, they beat me, Mother, and they threw me in the ditch with the dead
> They were all bleeding and I was covered with their blood
> Not my blood, Mother, but the blood of the dead Roma
> They threw them on top of me, Mother, the dead Roma
> The Germans killed them, Mother, and threw them in the ditch
> But I didn't die, Mother, I didn't die
> I lived to be alone in the world, alone among the Roma."

"That's a song from the death camps," I told Marie.

"They sound a lot like reservations," said Marie bitterly, "but the Germans were more merciful. It took only a few seconds with a bullet. Canada's taking generations to do it with my people."

Now the *Romungere* started singing a defiant battle song. It told of how they had secaped from the camps and joined the partisans; of the Nazis they had killed to avenge their dead families, and of the German women they had raped, and the German babies they had killed, so that they wouldn't grow up to be soldiers. They were savage Magyars now with the blood of warriors in their veins.

"Let's go, Marie," I said, "before the fight starts."

We made it just as a rumble started in one corner of the hall and spread as others rushed in to quell the violence.

It was now early evening and we strolled casually, hand in hand, along the street. Torontonians gaped at Marie's Gypsy costume. One guy in a leather jacket and bush boots just stood, dumbfounded, gawking at Marie.

"What's the matter with you, buddy?" she asked him. "You never seen a Gypsy Indian before? *Onege Wahi,*" she added, as he walked away.

"Who was that?" I asked her.

"Some guy just hit town from a reservation."

"Say," I told her, "you'd do great as a fortuneteller on the reservations."

"No, I wouldn't," she said. "We Indians don't have any future."

— 6 —

Marie and I left the small room we'd rented for the night and went back to the apartment building. Kolia and Tinka were gone but I found a note addressed to me on the table which said that Tinka's family had tracked Kolia down and were now in Toronto. I was to rejoin Kolia and his bride in Montreal where he had gone to place himself under the protection of the head patriarch of the Kalderash Gypsies in Canada.

Kolia went on to say that he'd left enough money for the bus fare to Montreal with old Shandor, the Hungarian Gypsy leader.

Marie changed out of her Gypsy dress and we packed our stuff, left the room and went downstairs to see the old patriarch. Jilko was with him. He gave us the money, wished us luck and we came back upstairs with Jilko.

"Vere you go now, Yanko?" Jilko asked.

"To Montreal, to Kolia and his family," I told him.

"Good," he smiled. "I go vit you. Dis town not good for me. I got car. I drive you."

We were just leaving when in walked half a dozen boys and young men, relatives of Tinka's. Jilko slipped past them and vanished up the hallway as they began searching the room.

"*Kai e Tinka?*" one of them asked belligerently. "You'd better tell us."

The voice was pitched and excited. I glanced past the intruders now gathered around Marie and I saw the old patriarch standing in the doorway with about a dozen of his followers. He said something in Hungarian and the Magyars grabbed Tinka's relatives and started propelling them forcibly from the room, heading for the stairs. One wild-looking fellow pulled a switchblade knife from his pocket, flicked open the blade and looked menacingly at the American Gypsies.

"*Nem szabad*," the old man said sternly, and the Romungero reluctantly put it back in his pocket.

"We warned Kolia," the old man said to me. "These American-born Gypsies are losing their own laws. They take the worst habits of the *Gazhe* and lose the best of their own. Go with God," he added, "my men will see you safely to the car."

I heard the sounds of scuffling on the stairs, American Gypsy insults in English countered by virulent Hungarian oaths, then the sound of ripping clothes followed by the multiple thuds of bodies moving down to the street. The Hungarian Gypsies returned and helped us carry out our luggage which we piled into Jilko's car.

"She run good," Jilko explained proudly as I stared in horror at the old jalopy. We got in and drove off.

"Ve go first and get my *lavuta*," Jilko told me as he drove into an expensive neighbourhood and stopped in front of a high-class modern apartment building, got out and walked to the entrance.

"Christ," I thought, surely he doesn't live here.

He rang the doorbell, nobody answered, then he glanced quickly up and down the street before producing a key to open the door. He vanished inside, closing the door behind him, then emerged a few minutes later carrying a violin case under his arm. He gave the violin to Marie who was sitting in the rear seat, and we drove off again.

"Dat good *lavuta*," he explained, "is vorth five tousan' dollar, maybe. Is lonk time I know dis rich *Gadjo* who have good fiddle. Now she mine. I go play night club in Montreal. French people is like Magyar music. I make big money, ve drink every night."

Jilko drove more or less in the direction of Montreal and I fell asleep. Jilko woke me up, much later; he'd taken a wrong turn somewhere and was now hopelessly lost on the south shore.

"Let me take the wheel," I told him. "I'll find out where we are and get back onto the main highway for Montreal."

Marie looked out of the window.

"I know where we are," she said proudly. "This is Indian land, Caughnawaga."

"That's right across from Lachine," I said. "Now I know how to get into the city. But, how did you know this was Indian land?"

"What did you just see out of the window?"

"Not much," I said. "Just a few old wooden shacks with little wooden toilets beside them."

Marie pointed out the window. "Almost everybody in Canada's got flush toilets except Indians. It keeps them busy filling up the holes; there's not much else to do on the reservation except to go to church on Sundays."

We passed through a more built-up area of the reservation, the part the tourists see as they speed along the super highway. It was now late summer and the leaves would soon be falling, then the dreaded winter would be upon us. This was always a time of hardship and suffering for the Gypsies. They hated the winter and most of them tried to earn enough during the summer months to last them through the winter.

It was getting dark as we approached Montreal along the south shore. For miles along the river, the lights stretched as far back as the eye could see. No other city in North America looks like Montreal. The old cross shone from the top of Mount Royal, Christian and aloof from the corruption, violence and beauty below it. I drove over the Jacques Cartier bridge past St. Helen's Island. By ten thirty we reached the store on St. Urbain just below Demontigny where Kolia and I were living with his parents. Behind this combination house-store was a yard surrounded on three sides by buildings and on the fourth by a high wall with a gate that led into a narrow lane.

This yard was our workshop where we plated basins and did other jobs. It was littered with singed rags, bits of metal and empty propane tanks.

A few French-Canadian housewives were sitting in two's and three's on the stairs of their flats, drinking beer and gossipping, haggard and sloppy, their bodies ruined from bearing too many children. They stared at Marie's neat figure as we climbed the unsteady wooden stairs and went through the ever-unlocked door into the house. Kolia, his parents, the Demitro patriarch, and a group of Roms were sitting around the table talking. I didn't see Tinka anywhere. They were having a *diwano*, or informal meeting, to discuss the problem of Kolia's elopement and what legal steps to take. Kolia had thrown himself on the mercy of the *Kris Romani*, or Gypsy court, and would abide by its decision.

Old Doikitsa greeted us. I introduced her to Jilko and Marie; she led us over to a smaller table, gave us a glass of tea each and went to the stove to warm up some food.

The *diwano* came to an end and most of the guests left, saying a courteous goodnight, but the old Demitro patriarch and another younger Gypsy and his wife remained, talking to Kolia and his father. I learned that just in case her father tried to take her back by force, Tinka was staying with Demitro's family until the matter had been settled.

We joined the others at the main table and the old lady brought us a plate each of *sarmi*, with a side dish of rice. Marie seemed shy to eat and kept chasing the flies off her food; the Gypsies were used to these uninvited guests. I ate with relish but took frequent gulps from the beer Kolia gave me. The food was over-spiced as usual. Jilko ate like a starving man; he hadn't eaten since the wedding. I told Kolia about the trouble with Tinka's relatives in the rooming house.

"*Carrajo,*" he said. "I wish I'd been there."

Suddenly, the door was thrown open and a group of men entered the house. It was Tinka's father, brothers, and other male relatives. They started arguing with Kolia's father, demanding the bridal price for Tinka and insulting Kolia. The old Demitro patriarch got up, his face serious, his voice full of authority. This was the man, years ago, who had challenged "Nigger Jack," the so-called crime king of St. Lawrence Main, for the right of Gypsies to open fortunetelling parlours on St. Lawrence Boulevard. Demitro and the huge black man had walked into the alleyway while a crowd of Gypsies, Blacks, petty hoods and other St. Lawrence Main characters stood in the entrance. Demitro had walked out, the other guy had been carried out and the Gypsies had been on the Main ever since.

"*Romale,*" Demitro said calmly. "Kolia is under the protection of the *Kris Romani.* Sit down and talk like men."

The intruders suddenly realized who was talking and assumed a much more peaceful tone though they still didn't sit down. Then Tinka's father got carried away again and started a vile tirade against Kolia's family, calling them all the foul names he could think of, even insulting their dead.

Old Valodia suddenly became years younger. He rushed at Tinka's father, slugged him in the stomach, knocked him prostrate on the floor and picked up a chair to brain him with as he struggled to get to his feet.

"*Kurav tu ando mui,*" he yelled, "I screw you in the mouth."

Kolia grabbed his arm before the chair descended.

"Gentlemen," Demitro called out. "Blows have been struck under a man's roof. Now this is a matter for the *Kris Romani.*"

Tinka's father turned pale as one of his burly sons helped him to his feet. He'd already prejudiced himself in the eyes of the court and Demitro was the supreme judge. He mumbled his apologies and left with his entourage. Order was soon restored. Kolia's mother started showing Marie around the house, explaining as best she could in her limited French all about the towels and soaps and other aspects of ritualistic cleanliness. I joined old Demitro on the couch and asked him what I should do about Marie. It's not an easy thing to bring an outsider into the Romani nation.

"Marry her," he told me. "By Gypsy law. Some of our men have married *Gazhya,* even two of my own sons."

"But who'll marry us, Uncle?" I asked, using the term *kak* for uncle, the formal address to a Gypsy patriarch.

"I will," he said. "If you want me to. Any patriarch can marry you. I'd be only too happy to perform the ceremony."

Kolia and his parents prepared the table and Demitro gave us the bread and salt. Jilko went around the corner to the bootlegger with a young Gypsy man and returned with some cases of beer and a bottle of wine. Marie and I drank a small glass of wine from the same glass, then I smashed it and passed the bottle around. Somehow I still didn't feel married; I wanted something more, something for Marie that would make her feel that we shared something more than this alien Gypsy ceremony. I did something that isn't part of the Gypsy culture although many non-Gypsy writers claim it to be.

"Kolia," I said, "come here."

I drew my bowie knife from the sheath inside my boot and handed it to him.

"You know what to do with this, *wortako,*" I told him. "You've known a lot of artists."

He smiled and made the incisions in Marie's and my wrists. He cut deep and I rubbed cigarette ash into the cuts before applying the bandaids. Wedding rings can be removed, even the *diklo,* the Gypsy women's head scarf and symbol of the wife, can be taken off but these scars would go with us to the grave.

"Why did you do that, Yanko?" Demitro asked me.

53

"I'm a sentimental fool," I told him.

His old eyes twinkled but he said nothing.

Old Valodia suddenly noticed Jilko's violin.

"You, Hungarian Rom," he called out. "Make some music."

Jilko took his fiddle tenderly out of the case and started playing the plaintive melodies of his people. He lost himself in his music and I began to see him as he really was, the sad little midget in a world of giants. He was too small for most women to notice but big enough not to let it get the better of him.

The party continued as more Gypsies dropped in bringing their instruments and cases of beer. Finally, everybody left and we all went to bed. Marie was soon asleep and as I drifted off, I heard the eternal scratching in the walls. I made a mental note to remind Kolia, tomorrow, to get a cat before those damned rats gnawed their way into the house.

— 7 —

Next day, Kolia and his parents left early in the afternoon to attend another *diwano* where the problem of the elopement would again be discussed. This time, Tinka's father would be there as well. Jilko went with another Hungarian Gypsy to look for a job as a violinist and I was left alone with my new wife.

Now that Kolia had a wife to run the house, we would take a place of our own somewhere nearby. Two women in the same house seldom get along together. Marie was wearing her Gypsy outfit and I told her that she'd make a good fortuneteller.

"Do these Gypsy women really know how to foretell the future?" she asked me.

"I really don't know," I said. "Most of the young ones, like Tinka just rattle off a spiel for their five bucks. They invent a lot of pleasant facts for their clients. But some of the older women like Kolia's mother, seem to have a certain insight; they scare me sometimes. Their observations and prophecies have a disturbing habit of coming true, especially those who know the Tarot."

"What's the Tarot?" she asked.

I went over to my suitcase and removed a bundle wrapped in my mother's faded yellow *diklo*, untied it and laid out a set of large and very old hand-painted cards on the floor. They were striking representations of demons, gods, and symbols.

"Christ," Marie gasped as the bold, forceful power of the long dead Gypsy artist reached across the years. She picked them up, one by one and studied them, fascinated. She had that same look as my own mother and I knew now, that she was the one I had carried them for.

"That's the Tarot," I told her, "at least part of it, the twenty-two arcana plus the seven keys of life. I have the minors, too, in

57

my suitcase."

"Do you understand them?" she asked.

"Each card portrays a certain span of human history," I told her. "If you know history, they all fit into a chronological time chart. This is the age we're in now and there's only one left."

I showed her a card with a man dressed as a court jester chasing a butterfly while a mad dog was running after him and ripping the seat from his trousers. He was absorbed with his elusive butterfly and didn't see the yawning precipice just ahead of him. This was arcanum 21, 20th century man.

"This is the last age," I went on. "It's going to start soon." It was a snake wrapped around an egg.

"The beginning of the end or the end of the beginning," I said. "The collapse of a civilization based on power and capital instead of on intellect and wisdom."

"Where did you get these things?"

"From my mother," I told her. "After she died, when I was fifteen, I went through her stuff before I moved out. I found these cards and that old leather stick you see standing up there over the bed. The old people were impressed with these things, but Kolia told me to hang the stick up there to scare away intruders. There's always drunks staggering in here; they mistake the place for a whorehouse."

"What a terrible thought," she said.

I wrapped up the cards and gave them to her. "Your wedding present," I told her.

She put them away and we went out for a walk, strolling hand in hand up to Sherbrooke Street and along to the Swiss Hut, a combination restaurant and bar with solid wooden tables and benches divided into separate booths in two sections, a square side and a beat side, segregation at the intellectual level. Kolia and I often bugged the waiters by changing sides as we felt like it. One night we'd sit with the painters, sculptors, and would-be writers on the beat side and another night we'd sit with some hood, detective, horny widow or old pensioner on the other. Now it was early afternoon and the place was deserted.

After our meal we decided to look for a place to live. We soon found one on Jeanne Mance just below Pine, on the third floor of a rooming house. We took a large double room facing onto the street below, a smaller room beside it that I could use as a studio, and workshop which had a gallery outside over the street. The kitchen and bathroom we shared with the other tenants. The place was basically furnished, and we could always go down to the Salvation Army on Notre Dame and get some more stuff later. I paid two weeks rent and we went back to Kolia's place to find that they'd all returned from the meeting. Tinka's father had asked for a *kris*, a regular assembly of Gypsy elders and a formal trial. It was his money or his daughter, he wouldn't settle for anything else. Three thousand dollars is what Kolia would have to pay to get Tinka legally.

Christ, I thought, he could have a lifetime of nookie on the Main for that much loot. Demitro could impose a certain time limit, say six months, in which the money must be paid. But if it wasn't, Tinka's father could legally reclaim his daughter, take her back and impose a heavy fine on Kolia's father.

I told Kolia about the place we'd rented and he seemed hurt to hear that we weren't planning to live with him.

"If Marie lives with Tinka," I explained, "Tinka will dominate her and keep her busy doing nothing all day. Marie wants to work so we can save some money."

"True," Kolia agreed, "your wife isn't a Gypsy woman. She wouldn't know how to defend herself with Tinka."

Kolia himself could do nothing. Gypsy men stay out of the domestic affairs of their womenfolk.

We collected our luggage and Kolia drove us to the place we'd rented. We had a few beers from the bag he brought, a sort of housewarming ceremony; then he went home, telling me to drop in early the following morning so we could look for jobs in the city.

Marie and I spent the rest of the day fixing up the place and making a list of the things we needed. By then, it was around eight P.M. and I suggested that we take a walk over to my friend Stan's place on Hutchison a few blocks away.

I'd left my stuff with him three years ago after Alec left for Europe and I decided to hitchhike out west and didn't quite make it as I met Kolia on the way.

I wanted to resume my model ship building. Marie would work until we had enough to rent a good flat or house.

Stan wasn't home but there was a party going on at his place. This wasn't unusual as I remembered he drove a taxi in the evenings to earn his living. I met a guy called Earl, the assistant editor of a university paper whom I remembered from the old days. This was the guy who'd condemned Alec for going overboard with his beatnik stuff. He'd forgotten my name.

"Lee," I told him. "Ron Lee, Alec's friend."

"Oh, yes," he smiled weakly. "I remember you now, you're the shipbuilder."

Stan's current chick told me that there was a letter for me from Alec. They'd kept it just in case I ever showed up again. It had a French stamp and a Paris postmark. I read it and burst out laughing as I handed it to Marie.

"Poor Alec," I said. "Hemingway goes over to Europe to serve in a worthy cause, Lennie Cohen goes there and learns Greek, but Alec, all he does is go there and catch himself a dose. Christ, he could have done that right here."

More guests arrived, Kolia among them.

"Yanko," he told me, "they told me in the Swiss Hut that you were over here. We have a job to do right away; it's worth about three hundred dollars but we need some strong men to help us move a large steam jacket boiler."

I looked at the mob of emaciated and dissipated young swingers. No good. We'd need an army of guys like this.

"Let's go over to El Cortijo on Clark Street and get some weight lifters and physical culture guys that hang around there," I suggested. "For a few bucks they'd help us move the Sun Life Building."

Kolia, Marie and I went over to El Cortijo and got four enormous brutes to help us. Then Kolia drove to a large candy factory where we took the elevator up to the fourth floor and entered an area with trays of candies in various stages of completion. The bodies beautiful began helping themselves to the delicacies as we studied the *damfo*, or steam jacket boiler. It was made of copper, like the two halves of a lemon, with a thick rim around the middle where the two halves were joined. It had a sort of door or hatch on the top and looked to me like the first submarine ever built, Bushnell's *Turtle* turned upside down with its screws and rudder removed, and a thick rim added around the middle.

Apparently it had sprung a leak under the rim allowing the pressure to dissipate.

"Is it a big job?" I asked Kolia.

"For the *Gazhe*, yes. For us, no," came his reply.

60

With the aid of a dolly, we somehow manhandled the monster over to the elevator. The trip down was the easiest part; then we sort of rolled and pushed it across the yard to our station wagon. After much grunting and a barrage of French-Canadian oaths from the strongmen, we had it resting on the open bottom of the trunk, lashed in position with ropes and chains, half in and half out of the wagon.

"*Maintenant à la maison*," Kolia said to the wrestlers.

We all piled into the car as the French-Canadians made jokes about "*cette maudite grande patente.*"

Once back home we got some chains, and the grunting, swearing, and panting started again. With some pushing and some pulling and Marie at the end of the chain we finally got the thing up the stairs, through the living room, past the mutterings of old Doikitsa who had visions of the floor caving in and Tinka, who hopped around it with dollar signs in her eyes. It finally came to rest in the kitchen where we would do the work.

Kolia opened a case of beer and gave the helpers a well-deserved drink as we all sat in the living room.

"How do we get it back?" I asked him.

He smiled. "We don't. They want the steam jacket boiler repaired, we want the work. When it's ready, they'll pick it up fast enough."

The weight lifters left after Kolia gave them ten bucks and we went into the kitchen to do the job. Kolia lit the gas jets on the large kitchen stove, put his soldering iron over one of them to heat up and a crucible full of soft copper over another to melt. Marie stood nearby, watching us, obviously intrigued. Then we turned the boiler on its side and Kolia heated the inside with his propane torch through the open hatch. He applied a temporary patch inside and we turned the whole thing upright again. Then he took his soldering iron and melted solder into the rim, all the way round, after which he poured molten copper into the crack where the rim joined the boiler. Next we turned the boiler upside down and repeated the process on the underside of the rim. Finally, we turned it upright again and Kolia removed his temporary tin patch from the inside. This patch had prevented the molten copper from flowing inside the basin and had given it time to harden.

"It should be all right now," he told me. "But we won't know until they test it."

I borrowed the station wagon from Kolia, and Marie and I returned to Stan's place for my stuff just before dawn. I saw that all the lights were out but that meant nothing. Stan's place was at the end of a long hallway in the basement and, after midnight, both he and his numerous guests usually went in and out through an open window which was at street level just over the lawn, almost hidden from sight by a section of the apartment building. This way, he was able to avoid annoying his neighbours.

"Follow me," I told Marie, as I sprinted catlike across the grass and rolled into the apartment through the open window. There was a bed left there by Stan to cushion the fall of his guests as they arrived. The bed was there, like I figured, only there was somebody in it. I landed with a thud on top of someone who struggled to get up and made me lose my balance. I reached out, frantically in the darkness, for something to hang onto and found it. My strong coppersmith's hand locked itself firmly around a plump female breast. She didn't scream. It's hard to when there's somebody sitting on your stomach. A male voice nearby demanded to know what the hell was happening, but he was soon silenced into a gasp of agony as Marie landed on top of him.

"Christ, like man," I heard another male voice explode, followed by the sound of somebody staggering across the floor. Whoever it was stumbled and I heard a loud crash followed by a shrill female scream and the sound of bottles rolling on the floor. Somebody turned the lights on and the first thing I saw was Marie sitting with her legs apart, her dress hiked up around her waist exhibiting the stiletto on her thigh, while her sexy rump was resting on some guy's face. About a dozen people, mostly teenagers, were lying naked, or nearly so, around the room on sofas, on the floor and on the beds. Marie got off her victim and I saw that it was Earl, the assistant editor. He struggled to get up as I got off his also nude female partner.

"Oh, it's you, Ron," he said weakly as he sat there looking utterly ridiculous in his birthday suit. I saw a guy lying on the floor surrounded by beer bottles and I reconstructed what had happened. He must have got up to put the light on, bumped into the table and knocked it over scattering the bottles and half-finished glasses of beer.

"For Christ's sake put the friggin' lights out," a youngster ordered and a naked girl sprang to obey.

"Where's Stan?" I asked Earl.

"In his room with his chick," he told me. "He's got some stuff in there."

I took Marie by the hand and led her into Stan's bedroom. The table lamp was on and he and his chick were sitting on the floor, naked and smoking pot. Stan greeted me like he'd seen me only yesterday and told me all the local news. We talked while his chick got some beers for Stan and me, and a glass of wine for Marie. I heard the sounds of more people arriving and the noise of more bottles being opened. Somebody turned on the record player, jazz. Through the half-open door of Stan's bedroom I could see the beam of a flashlight playing around the room outside. Some clod was getting his kicks by exposing the couples in their love making and giggling insanely to himself.

A young man staggered into Stan's room wearing only his pants; he made for Stan's bed but about halfway across the room he suddenly clutched his stomach and crumpled slowly to the floor like a soldier cut down by machine gun fire. Stan covered him with a blanket.

"Rough trip," he told us. "He can sleep it off there."

Soon it was dawn and Stan came back to earth long enough to remember where my stuff was. We collected it and started to leave just as Earl passed us in the cold light of dawn, still naked and with a serious, determined look on his face and a glass of beer in his hand, and vanished into the washroom. We heard the violent sound of glass shattering on the tiled floor followed by the dull thud of his body, then, inhuman sounds of terrible retching, puking, and moaning. Christ, I thought, when will these punks learn that you can't mix liquor, pot, and acid.

Stan and his chick helped us carry my stuff through the apartment and out through the window.

"What terrible people," Marie said as we drove away. "Who are they?"

I reassured her. "They're only the satellites, hangers-on, poor little rich kids hitting back at daddy for giving them all the things that you and I never had, like a college education. Real beatniks, hippies, and artists are human beings with a philosophy and a way of life that has merit. Those young punks back there are nothing but a bunch of degenerates; Stan isn't, but they just use him and his pad."

I felt disgusted and decided to drive up the mountain to the lookout to fresh air and sanity. We sat on the grass near the top of the stairs leading down to the park below. The early morning sunshine broke through and showed us the city, the tall office buildings, the factories and the slums. Ships were moving in the Saint Lawrence and early morning traffic was beginning to flow into the city streets. I looked at the office complex where I had once worked. Long ago, I had stood at a window high up there and looked down at the people lying in the park below. Later, I'd lain in the park with Alec and stared at the pale faces looking down. Once later I'd returned with Kolia and done a job on the kitchen equipment of the staff cafeteria, and nobody recognized the swarthy "Spaniard" as Ronald Lee, the young clerk in the accounts receivable department who used to eat lunch in the second sitting.

I grabbed Marie and kissed her.

"*Ganarunkwah,*" I told her in her own language, "I love you."

"*Voliv tu ime,*" she replied in Romani, "I love you, too."

— 8 —

The next few months passed uneventfully as autumn drew on. I continued to work with Kolia. Marie, who was now pregnant, did some typing at home. She had no other skills but she'd found a legal firm that supplied her with regular work. Jilko had done O.K. for himself and was playing in a Hungarian restaurant-cabaret. He moved into the same rooming house as Marie and I.

Kolia turned the store front of his home into a real fortune-telling parlour with the required license for graphology. Fortune-telling was technically illegal in Quebec province, but in the slum areas where the Gypsies usually lived the police either ignored them completely or fined the women periodically for prostitution. A few of the Canadian-born Gypsy women had taken to picking pockets in their mitt-joints as did their American-born sisters and the police made little distinction between the genuine thieves and the honest, but illegal, fortunetellers. So a Gypsy woman would break the law by telling somebody's fortune, less often by taking a few bucks from his wallet, and the police would then arrest her for running a disorderly house. The judge would reprimand her for her life of sin while her husband paid the fine and pocketed his receipt. A few days later the same woman would be back again and the whole performance would be repeated. If she appeared too often in court she would eventually be given one of two generous alternatives: she could go to jail or leave town in a hurry. Naturally, she always chose the latter and both the law and the Gypsies knew that this merry-go-round could go on forever.

Kolia told Tinka not to do any stealing or swindling in the store. The sexy feel-up wallet-grabbing routine of some of the Canadian-born Gypsy women was distasteful to him, as it was to all European-born Gypsies. Old Demitro himself had told the women under his sphere of influence not to take up these rackets but some ignored him. They would never try them in his presence, but the old fellow wasn't ubiquitous.

Finding a suitable workshop for the coming winter created another problem. Our shop in the backyard would be out of the question when buried under six feet of snow, so we found a garage, rented it, and turned it into a tolerable indoor workshop.

Marie and I had fixed up our place comfortably and I now felt the urge to collect my ship model building tools and research data to set up a studio. I borrowed the car from Kolia and went with Marie to the home of my relative to collect what I'd left there before I met Kolia. He was a second cousin of my mother and lived in Montreal West. I phoned him to tell him we were coming and we arrived in the late afternoon. He greeted us warmly and brought us a drink after I'd introduced him to Marie and explained who she was and where I'd been for the last three years.

Marie saw my two completed ship models on his mantle-piece and studied them with interest; one was the *Ark Royal*, the other, the famous Canadian racing and fishing schooner, *Bluenose*. They were both complete in every detail, with hand-sewn sails and small figurines of the crew at a scale of 1:96.

My cousin and I gathered up the two trunks and the boxes full of books and material and piled it all on the floor.

Marie stared at the heap. "Do you need all that stuff just to make model ships?" she asked.

"Everything I need has to come from books—plans, rigging diagrams, even contemporary novels often have details that are useful. That pile of loose-leaf notebooks full of drawings I've done only goes from 1500 to 1600 and from 1700 to 1850. I still have to complete it."

"What are you going to do now, Ron?" my cousin asked me as he lit his pipe. "You have a wife expecting and no job."

"I'm working with one of the Kalderash Gypsies, Kolia Kwiek," I told him. "I make a fair living."

"For how long?" he asked. "I've heard of your association with the nomads. We still know what goes on among them even if we've left the road ourselves."

"I guess you do," I said. "Incognito Gypsies always manage to find out what the nomads are doing, but you've all crawled up your own arseholes and died trying to hide yourself from the *Gazhe*."

"We still know who we are," he argued.

"*Zhanes tu sar te hanos archichiesa?*—Do you know how to plate tin?"

There was no reply.

"You'll have to make your own decision," he said finally. "You can shut your mouth and pass as a *Gazho* if you want to. You can be anything in Canada, even Black or Indian like this young lady here, but they'll never let you be a Rom except on the road or in the slums with the rest of the Turks. If you want anything better for yourself you'll have to become incognito."

"*Rom sim tai Rom merava*—A Gypsy I am and a Gypsy I'll die," I said defiantly.

"You just might," he said, a little sadly. "The nomads haven't got long left. If you're known as a Gypsy, we run the risk of being associated with you, you know that. A lot of us have good jobs, we handle money, we're trusted because nobody knows what we are."

"Don't worry," I told him. "You're secret will be safe with me."

"What do you think, young lady?" he asked Marie.

She looked at him and answered in French. "*Quand on prend mari on prend pays.*"

He understood, but said nothing.

We loaded my stuff into the car and drove back to our small apartment. Later, we went down to El Cortijo where we were supposed to meet Jilko and Kolia.

By now it was early evening and we sat together at a table waiting for the others. Tonight was poetry night and the young poets had assembled to read. Whatever culture there is in Canada, is French.

Kolia appeared in the doorway and padded down the stairway, his primitive features contrasting vividly with those of the intellectuals around us.

A poet got onto the stage and started reading his masterpiece through the microphone, his face serious, his skinny hands clutching his papers, his uncombed beard matted and dirty.

"*Ma femme est morte, et moi, je suis libre,*" he read.

Kolia seemed annoyed by the poetry and looked impatiently around for a waiter. He saw Antonio standing at the far end of the hall.

"*Oyes, paisano,*" he yelled, "*Un café por favor.*"

The poet stopped in mid-sentence, everybody stared at Kolia but the Gypsy seemed completely unaware of his uncool act. This was a restaurant and he'd simply ordered a coffee from a waiter.

"*Ma femme est morte,*" the poet started off again.

"*Con leche,*" Kolia added.

Again silence.

The poet glared at Kolia. "*As-tu fini, Monsieur?*"

"*Quoi, so, que dice?*" Kolia seemed confused and had a look of genuine bewilderment on his face. Marie started laughing.

"*Bien,*" the poet said. "*Je commencerai de nouveau—avec votre permission.*"

Kolia now sat silent, trying to look interested.

"*Ma femme est morte, et moi, je suis libre,*" the poet began again.

Now Jilko appeared in the doorway carrying his fiddle under his arm and wearing a jaunty cap over his mop of black curly hair. He saw the poet and his Gypsy face twisted into a grin.

"*Dikes oda baro shero,*" he yelled to us in Hungarian Romani, "Look at that big show off!"

The poet threw his papers onto the stage.

"*Sacrement!*" he swore, "*Quelle sauvagerie. Ces maudits anglais.*"

Now I started laughing. Three Gypsies and an Indian woman. There wasn't an Englishman or even an English-Canadian in the place. Some of the customers also started to laugh.

"*Envoye,*" one of them yelled to Jilko. "*la musique tsigane!*"

Soon the poets were forgotten as the plaintive notes of Jilko's violin floated across the basement hall.

"That's better," Kolia said, "I was getting fed up with those poets."

After a while Jilko stopped playing and sat down with us to eat a meal, one of those long sandwiches, or *bocadillos*, they specialized in.

"Let's go over to the Hut," Kolia suggested. "I'm thirsty and they don't serve beer here."

We got in the car and drove over to the Swiss Hut. We drank beer, Marie wine. Kolia, normally a sober character, liked to have his periodic drinking bouts and Jilko, like most Hungarian Gypsies, liked his *shasto* or *mulatni*. By nine o'clock, a large group had assembled around the semicircular table on the beat side and Jilko's fiddle along with somebody's mouth organ provided us with musical accompaniment for the old French-Canadian folksongs like

C'est l'Aviron.

Then Jilko played Gypsy music and I got up and danced while the assembled painters, sculptors, writers, and would-be many things yelled their shouts of encouragement. Somebody let out with a wild yell. It was Marie. Wearing her wide Mexican skirt and embroidered bodice, her long black hair done Gypsy style with the eternal rose over her left ear, she started dancing on top of the table. Her high-heeled shoes made a staccato on the table top, spilling glasses and crushing the packages of cigarettes. The crowd clapped their hands and her skirt twirled, rose and showed us the stiletto on her thigh.

"Christ," I thought happily. "What savages we are." I realized, suddenly, that we were outlaws not because we were not Canadians, but because we were. Here were people of all origins, almost all of them born in Canada, barring the odd immigrant like Jilko or Kolia, enjoying themselves in an old frontier style get-together within sight of the skyscrapers and the synthetic entertainment of commercialized culture.

Later Jilko suggested that the four of us go to a Hungarian party he knew of, so we left and drove up Park Avenue into Park Extension and stopped in front of a five-story building. There seemed to be parties going on everywhere. I saw people entering one of the halls wearing masquerade costumes.

"Ve go second floor to Magyar party," Jilko told us.

The hall was crowded, many wore the Hungarian national costume. Some were dancing their national dances while others were sitting at the tables along the walls, talking and drinking. A Gypsy band was playing at the far end, on the stage. Above them was a large Hungarian flag of the pre-Communist era and underneath it, a sign, in English and presumably Hungarian, which said: "Hungary's freedom is your security."

I felt out of place here, as did Marie, but Kolia, as usual, had found somebody to talk to and Jilko was among his own people.

I noticed Kolia talking volubly to his new-found friend in a language that sounded to me like somebody trying to speak Spanish with a gag on and with his mouth full or marbles.

"The *Zenhor* is Portuguese," Kolia informed me, "a fellow countryman of mine from Lisboa."

Kolia conned the fat old Portuguese into buying a lot of liquor for our table. The *Zenhor* told us that there was a much better party going on upstairs so we decided to go there. We collected the liquor and stuffed it inside our jackets. Kolia and his new-found friend carried most of it, supporting each other and acting like a couple of drunks to hide the all-too-obvious bulges in their clothes. We passed the Hungarian doorman without any trouble but there was some kind of policeman with him who gave us a funny look. He was wearing a Mountie-style stetson, blue jacket, khaki jodhpurs, and high brown leather boots. He had bright shiny buttons, and a brand new holster for his revolver. In his hand, he held a riding whip. I noticed the silver spurs and wondered what the hell had happened to his horse. He stood erect, busy looking, important. It's all right to give a French-Canadian a uniform, but brass buttons are fatal.

We went upstairs to the masquerade party and found that English seemed to be the main language being spoken. It looked like some large corporation was having a gathering. We found a table and sat down. Marie was wearing her Gypsy-Mexican outfit plus a beaded Indian headband; I guessed she'd pass as something or other since most of the women we wearing costumes. The men wore mainly business suits or sports clothes so we didn't look too out of place. Kolia asked Marie to dance, the Portuguese vanished and I got into a conversation with a friendly guy sitting at the next table who was obviously quite drunk.

"Swell shindig, isn't it," he smiled.

"It sure is," I agreed.

"Have a cigar." He offered me a large box full of Havanas. I took one and he lit it for me with his lighter.

"There's a crazy contest going on here," he informed me. "They have a bunch of jokers planted in the audience to do crazy stunts, you know, something like Candid Camera. Nobody knows about it, but Harry told me. He knows I can keep a secret."

Kolia came back with Marie; he was hungry but there was no food left at the buffet. I looked around and saw that my friend, who had now gone to the washroom, had an enormous plate full of sandwiches, sausage rolls, cakes, and biscuits on the table for his group. I got a sudden inspiration and outlined my plan to Kolia in Romani. He left and vanished into the crowd.

My happy friend now returned and I introduced him to Marie. He sat down, took a swig of his whisky. Kolia appeared and spoke to him in English that sounded too broken to be genuine. He told the man that he was starving, that he was a poor immigrant with no job, a wife and eleven children, that there was no food in the house and that he must have something to eat before he collapsed from hunger.

The other people at my friend's table looked at Kolia abashed. Things like this don't happen in Canada.

"Take all this," my friend told Kolia, handing him the tray.

Kolia started stuffing the food inside a paper bag which he produced from his pocket.

"Is that enough?" the man asked.

"Yes," Kolia said. "Tank you very mooch."

"No, wait, have a cigar, take the whole damned box," the man added. He started cramming cigars into Kolia's pockets.

As Kolia walked away the man burst out laughing.

"Old Harry really came through this time," he told me. "Imagine that guy trying to pass as a D.P. His accent was too phoney. They should have picked real foreigners or actors. That guy was a dead giveaway. I'm sure I know him from somewhere. Insurance, I think. What will those guys think up next. It takes Harry and the boys to throw a real shindig. I still remember the time he brought those girls all the way from New York for Bill's stag. The guy should be a movie director."

Marie and I excused ourselves and went to meet Kolia and Jilko downstairs where they were busy eating their loot at the Hungarian party. The Portuguese stayed upstairs with a woman he'd met and we decided to leave as a fervent political discussion had just erupted in the Hungarian hall.

"Ve go now," Jilko advised us. "Soon is gonna be big trouble here."

Kolia wrapped up what was left and we got out just as the brawl broke out. I heard the savage screams and filthy oaths mingled with the sounds of breaking glass and rushing feet as the Magyars locked in conflict. We passed the police cruisers converging as we drove away. I wondered what happened to my pseudo-Mountie friend, alone in there with all those wild Hungarians and Gypsies.

We laughed like fools as we ate the food on our way back to Kolia's house. The old people were still up. We got some liquor from the bootlegger, phoned some of the other Gypsies, and soon we had a party going. Stevo, the mandolin player and his nephew, Jimmy, the guitarist, arrived along with many more. Tinka stayed wrapped in her quilts, grumbling and moaning about the noise. She couldn't enjoy herself and she didn't want anybody else to, either. But the old people made merry along with the rest of us. I felt happy as I watched the Gypsies singing and dancing, Marie along with them.

I got up and called to Jimmy.

"*De manga Baso,*" I yelled, "Give me Baso."

I danced, wildly, this Kalderash dance that Gypsies dance all over the world, making all the gestures of defiance. Marie joined me and the others yelled their shouts of encouragement. For hundreds of years, Roms have been dancing Baso and perhaps my grandson would be dancing it a hundred years hence. At that moment I felt somehow, come what may, the Gypsies would be among the last people to be dehumanized.

9

It was winter again.

Christmas had come and gone and the streets of Montreal were littered with abandoned Christmas trees, wreaths and other Yuletide decorations. Our workshop in the backyard looked like the North Pole, but at least the unsightly debris was hidden. Kolia's old station wagon was also frozen solid and buried under ice and snow in the municipal parking lot near El Cortijo.

It was cold in the house where he lived. The old stove did its best, but the wind just blew right through the cracks around the windows. Tinka had become something of a hypochondriac. She was very pregnant and passed the days keeping warm in bed, wrapped in a quilted eiderdown, while old Doikitsa tried gallantly to run the house. Kolia seemed invulnerable. He'd finally paid off Tinka's father and had now been embraced as a *zhamutro*, or son-in-law. Tinka wanted to go back to the States, to her family, but Kolia had misgivings. He still didn't speak much English and thought that he'd find it difficult to work there. Not that Tinka's family did much anyway. The men were mostly on public welfare and the women earned the big money through their rackets: witchcraft swindles and fortunetelling.

There wasn't much work in Montreal for Kolia and he spent his time sitting at the living room table studying maps of Quebec and Ontario, trying to work out a route for the coming spring, writing down the towns where he hadn't yet been. Like all nomadic Gypsies, he hated to be idle.

Actually, Kolia couldn't read in the sense that he could form words, but like many of his people, he saw the printed word as a pictogram and had grown familiar with the names of cities, streets, signs denoting public washrooms and highway markers. Thus he was able to pick out towns without difficulty and then, laboriously to transcribe their names on his list, holding the pencil the same way he held the scriber when marking sheets of copper.

I had been working for a large department store as a Christmas extra while Marie stayed home and did her typing assignments. It had been fun selling electric trains, model soldiers and plastic kits. But I got fed up chasing away kids.

"*Touche-les pas*," a haggard mother would say to some eager little Jacques or Pierre as he caressed an expensive teddy bear or battery-operated squirrel. "*Touche-les pas, c'est pas pour nous autres.*"

Today I'd been laid off. Business was back to its normal January low.

I tried to get a regular job. They were polite in the employment offices and took the time to read all my references up to the last job I'd worked at.

They would smile approvingly and then ask me the fatal question.

"And where have you worked for the last five years, Mr. Lee?"

What could I tell them? That I'd gone beat for a while, then worked with an itinerant Gypsy coppersmith, that I'd been unemployed, in the army? Over three years of my working life were missing, a complete blank. It was as if I'd been in jail; this is what they may have thought but weren't honest enough to ask. I realized now I was an employment risk and condemned to part-time or low-salaried jobs.

The full impact of it finally hit me. Like Kolia and Jilko, I was an outlaw, a person without roots or records of his unbroken history of employment. Like any other Canadian drifter, ex-con or ex-alcoholic who was trying to get back into society to earn a living, I was branded and all doors were locked. My friend Alec had prophesied it that day I left my wife Linda to move in with him, "There's no way back."

So Gypsy I would be and like the rest of my cursed people, do what I had to to survive. By choosing this life I'd burned my bridges behind me. For myself, I could starve as well as the next guy but I was no longer alone. Soon, a half-Indian, half-Gypsy kid would be born and that meant the poor little bastard already had a sixty percent handicap against him in his own country. I felt that I'd have to even those odds.

I thought as I walked along St. Catherine Street towards Kolia's place, "I'll make it someday now that I have Marie to help me." But would I?

I was convinced that I had ability and enough training to be a successful ship model builder or maritime historian with some museum and I had other specialized talents that should be worth something, like the five languages I spoke fluently. The trouble was to convince the right people. What chance did I really have, I thought, a member of an off-white minority group without backing and nepotic connections? Gypsies aren't ship model builders; for that you have to be an ex-admiral of the fleet or the son of a retired sea captain. Gypsies aren't artists, they're fortunetellers or violin players like Jilko, horse thieves or knife-wielding avengers of the slurs against their women. Whoever heard of a Gypsy expert on maritime history and naval architecture?

I knew it wasn't a matter of talent. That's the thing you need least in Canada where art is a matter of the emperor's new clothes. The business world took the attitude of "How little can I pay for this, and how much can I sell it for?"

I almost wished I'd been a wrestler, hockey player or even a champion masturbator, or perhaps, like Marie had told me, "They should recognize good lovers, you'd have it made, buddy." Yes that probably was the one realm where the "native" does excel the white man, the only time he has an equal chance to compete honestly without handicaps.

Maybe Kolia would become wealthy, I speculated, the owner of a plant manufacturing prophylactics, sanitary napkins or toothpicks and push me all the way to the top through his powerful influence among his fellows in the Rotary Club, Chamber of Commerce, Historical Society and the corner whorehouse.

But no, I wouldn't wish such a fate on poor old Kolia. I preferred to see him singing his old Kalderash melodies in the Swiss Hut.

I reached Kolia's house and ran up the stairs. I found him talking with Jilko who was still wearing his heavy nylon ski jacket. The old people were in bed but old Doikitsa got up to make some tea.

"Don't bother, auntie," I told her. "I just ate."

But she insisted. If she died doing it, her guest would have his tea according to the code of hospitality of the Gypsies.

Tinka, who should have got the tea, was lying in bed smothered by quilts. She kept moaning to herself. "*Yoi, Devla, me merava*—Oh

God, I'm dying."

Why didn't she die and get it over with? She was certainly no sicker than Kolia's parents and *they* never complained. They knew that Kolia was doing his best. Nobody would rent a decent house to people like us. The constant repairing of vats and mixing bowls in the backyard wouldn't be tolerated anywhere but in these slums. In truth, the owner probably couldn't care less if Kolia did set fire to the house with his blowtorch; it would save him the expense of having it demolished in a year or so to make way for expensive highrise sardine can apartments.

The old lady brought me my tea, already cold. Kolia told me that he'd just found a small job to do in the city. Tinka got up from the bed and made her way painfully across the room heading for the bathroom. What an actress, I thought, she should try for Hollywood. There was nothing wrong with her except that like Marie, she was pregnant. But she kept telling Kolia to call the doctors to give her painkilling drugs and sleeping pills. She would gulp down a week's supply. I tried to tell Kolia that she was becoming a dope addict but he wouldn't believe me. He was a European Gypsy and among his people nobody said they were sick unless they really were. He just kept on paying for the pills and Tinka kept on taking advantage of him.

She finally reached the bathroom, went inside and closed the door behind her. A few minutes later I heard her scream with terror. She rushed out of the toilet, sprinted across the room like a trained athlete and sprang into bed yelling hysterically.

"Kolia, there's a rat in the toiler bowl!"

Kolia, Jilko and I went into the bathroom and saw a large rat struggling in the bowl alongside Tinka's turd. It must have come up the sewage pipes. Kolia rushed into the kitchen, got his *kleshto* and grabbed the rat in the middle of its back. As he picked it up, it turned its head and bit savagely at the tongs, its ugly face contorted with rage and pain. Kolia carried it through the house to the back door leading onto the balcony over the yard below, opened the door and threw the rat over the railings of the gallery. It landed heavily and sank into the soft snow near the bags of garbage piled up just inside the gate. It struggled onto the hard surface of the surrounding frozen snow and tried to escape but it was jumped by the gang of alley-cats that had been busy attacking the garbage bags. In a few seconds they had torn it to pieces and we could see its guts and fur scattered all over the snow. One old brown cat wrested the head away from a smaller white one and made off with it, hotly pursued by two more.

Jilko looked pale, like he wanted to puke. Kolia said nothing. What a scene, I thought. Brutal, terrible and Canadian.

We went back inside the house and took a good slug of brandy each. "To get warm," Kolia explained to the others.

Tinka was now sobbing and moaning and I thought of Alec's possible comment. "What's she so excited about?" he'd probably say. "Think if it were you or I who'd gone in there. The *shmaltser* might have bitten our pecker off." Only the seriousness of the situation stopped me from laughing aloud.

As the day wore on, Tinka got worse. She started to get real pains and I sent Jilko to get Marie since it was obvious that she was going into labour.

"Get a doctor right away," Marie told us.

Kolia went to the corner store and tried. He came back frightened. "I can't get one," he said, desperate.

"Call the police," I told him. "No doctor will come to this part of the city, you know that."

The cops arrived and got Tinka into the police ambulance. They turned on the siren and rushed her to the hospital. We followed in a taxi. She was immediately taken into an operating room. We waited downstairs until a doctor came down.

"Your wife's all right," he told Kolia, "but we couldn't save the baby."

"*Che choromos,*" Kolia moaned aloud, "what misery." He was completely demoralized.

We took a taxi back to my apartment. Jilko went for some beer and Kolia started drinking heavily. "Let him get stoned," I thought. "If he passes out, he can sleep it off here. Jilko or I can stay with the old people for the night."

I'd never seen Kolia this disturbed before. Like all nomadic Gypsies, he was fully convinced of the existence of God and held many other religious and mythological beliefs. He kept asking why God had smitten him and what he'd done wrong to offend Him. He cursed himself for having broken some divine or Gypsy law.

I'd always envied Kolia for his simple strength and his primitive wisdom, I'd felt that he was somehow stronger than I was. Now I realized as I watched him that my education had been of some help. To me, it was purely a matter of medical science; but to him, it was some unfathomable tragedy, another example of divine punishment that had been descending on his large family ever since his extended family members had been arrested and murdered by the Nazis in Poland. Eventually he fell asleep on the couch, and Jilko went down to stay with the old people.

Next morning we went back to the hospital. The doctors wanted to keep Tinka there, but she insisted on leaving. So we bundled her into a taxi and went to Kolia's house. His mother was crying. Tinka kept staring at Marie's stomach where she knew there was another baby about the age of the one she'd just lost.

Nobody said much. Tinka was for going back to the States right away, with or without Kolia and his parents, and finally Kolia, docile and bending as usual, agreed to go with her.

"But Kolia, the car's frozen in the lot," I argued.

"*Ankalavas*," he said grimly, "we'll get it out."

After changing the battery and struggling for an hour we finally got the old heap started. By the time we returned, the old people had packed and we loaded everything into the station wagon. The old people sat in the back with Tinka, huddled under a pile of quilts and blankets. Jilko joined Kolia in the front.

"I go vit you, my friend," he said to Kolia. "Is too long way for von man. I drive too. Ve go Chicago, I see Hungarian Gypsy people there. I come back to Yanko in Montreal in bus."

I couldn't say much as Kolia started the motor. He looked at me, his face emotionless. Only his eyes told of his deep sorrow.

"Stay with God, Yanko my brother," he said.

"Go with God," I replied.

I shook hands with his father and said goodby to the old lady. She looked like a mother eagle as she hovered over Tinka. They drove off and we waved to them until the car disappeared.

Marie and I stood in front of the old house. It was cold and we had about thirty-five dollars between us. I had no job and there were still several months of winter ahead. My only sure method of earning a living had just now ceased with Kolia's departure.

We walked slowly over to El Cortijo, hand in hand. Somebody had written a slogan on the wall outside in white paint.

"*Vive le Québec libre.*"

"Come on, Marie." I patted her stomach. "We're all getting cold out here."

O bengoro is the lesser devil or carnalized man, the man who has allowed himself to become corrupted by the environment around him. This is the world of hedonism, of vice, duplicity, dishonesty and self-abasement. In the picture we see *O buzno*, the he-goat and ruler of the Black Mass. It signifies the man who rejects the esthetic, mystical and artistic values of humanity.

This is the world Yanko finds in the slums into which he is forced along with the remnants of his people in Canada.

10

And so the years passed. It was now the summer of 1965 and I was doing my rounds in Montreal, selling Hindu handicrafts for an Indian importer. Kolia was still in the States with Tinka's family but Jilko had returned and was living with Marie and me in a rooming house on Jeanne Mance. He was playing in the clubs and cabarets, but there wasn't too much demand now for Hungarian Gypsy music.

I was walking along St. Catherine Street near the Forum when I saw a Gypsy mitt-joint that must have just opened. I went into the store. A fat, blond woman was sitting on the sofa in the front part. I could hear voices speaking in Romani on the other side behind the curtains. I studied the woman for a moment. She was wearing the traditional long Gypsy skirt, blouse and gold-painted slippers. At first I thought she might be a non-Gypsy, but then I saw her eyes and decided she was a half-Gypsy.

"You want a reading, mister?" she asked. She got up from the sofa and came towards me as another smaller, dark-skinned Gypsy woman came out from behind the curtains and edged around behind me, trying to get at my wallet.

"*Kon san tume?*" I asked in Romani, "Who are you? Do you take me to be a bloody *Gazho*?"

When they heard me speaking Romani, they stopped. "We are of the Burt family," the dark woman told me.

The Burtya, or Burts, was one of the two large Canadian Gypsy clans; the other was Demitro.

A man appeared from behind the drapes. He was heavy set and powerfully built, expensively dressed, his hands adorned with numerous gold rings. He also sported a gold tie pin, a watch chain, many gold teeth and a savage-looking moustache. It was Burtya, whom I'd met many times at Gypsy feasts, weddings and meetings. I now guessed who the women were. The big blond must be his sister Besserabia, the powerful he-woman who'd married a little runt of a guy. The other Gypsies called him her *romoritsa*, sticking a feminine diminutive onto a male noun, *Rom*, meaning husband or married Gypsy man. He was a weak little frump who wore an apron, did the housework, cooked the meals, changed the diapers and generally played a submissive feminine role. She made the money by telling fortunes and picking pockets. The smaller, dark woman must be Pavlena, Burtya's wife.

He greeted me. "*Sar mai san?*" he said, "How are you? I've opened the city again. We're moving back in from Toronto."

By "opened", he meant that he'd been down to City Hall and paid somebody off to get a certain number of permits issued to the various family groups under his influence. This would enable them to sell horoscopes and trinkets and dabble at phrenology as a legitimate front for their fortunetelling.

"I told 'em to go slow," he added, "no rough stuff, just honest fortunetelling and pickpocketing and maybe a little swindling if the loot is worth it. No use burning up the town for nothing. I've warned them. I opened the town again," he concluded grimly, "and I'll close it if anybody gets out of line."

He was about as close to being a chieftain as any Gypsy can be. He and old Demitro were the two big wheels among the Canadian-born Gypsies. They had fought each other for years, each trying to outsmart and get the better of the other, even though Burtya's wife, Pavlena, was Demitro's sister. The two leaders were officially on speaking terms and their fighting consisted of Machiavellian backstabbing and squealing on each other to thepolice. Violence had actually occurred in the past over rights of territory. Only so many Gypsies can operate in the same town and these two guys and their clans always wanted to be in the same town.

Demitro was much older than Burtya, much wiser and more philosophical. Burtya was stronger, more pragmatic and violent. Demitro could read and write; Burtya was illiterate. Each ruled his respective *vitsa*, or clan, in his own way and each clan had managed to survive and multiply in Canada. Demitro thought more like a European Gypsy and tried to make his people follow the older, more honest ways. Burtya, on the other hand, was Canadianized and ready to try any swindle or penny-ante racket if he thought he could get away with it by paying off somebody somewhere. There were also immigrant Gypsies like Kolia's people or visitors from the States, who don't belong to either of these two Canadian groups, but the Burts and the Demitros with their assorted sub-families of Stokes, Markovitch, Wilson, Mitchell, Miller and others all owed nominal allegiance to one of these two *kaks*, or uncles.

"Is your brother-in-law in town?" I asked Burtya.

He knew whom I meant. It was well-known among the Gypsies that I had become a sort of general-secretary to old Demitro who was fighting a losing battle to get certain petty by-laws altered or new statutes introduced that would enable the Canadian-born Gypsies to make an honest living within the framework of their traditions and way of life.

"He moved in a few days ago," Burtya told me. "He's living with his son, Charlie. You know him, Gypsy Charlie, the fence over on Charlotte Street next to the cathouse. He's been there for years."

"Thanks," I said. "By the way, do you want any nice Hindu saris or brass decorations?"

"*Haide palal*," Burtya ordered, as he went behind the curtains.

I picked up my case and followed him, along with the two women. I was surprised to see a uniformed constable sitting alone at the family table obviously enjoying a good Gypsy meal of stuffed cabbage rolls, a side dish of rice and a bottle of beer. I opened my sample case and showed them my wares.

"That's not *marime*, is it?" Burtya asked, motioning towards the saris, which meant that if some woman had worn them he would be automatically defiled under Gypsy law by touching them.

"They're brand new," I told him.

The two women admired the saris. Besserabia wanted to buy one but my samples were useless; Hindu women don't come that big. Pavlena took one; she was small and fine-boned. Burtya bought a brass ashtray shaped like a frog; he looked at it for a minute.

"How's that D.P. Gypsy friend of yours, Kolia?" he asked. Obviously the frog had reminded him of the *Brashka*, Kolia's mother-in-law.

"He's still in the States," I told him. "Almost five years now."

They wanted more stuff, but with my own people my business was always cash and carry. Gypsies always intend to pay back money they owe but their hand-to-mouth existence usually prevents it.

I left the store and took a bus east to St. Lawrence. Then I walked along to Berger, turned down and left onto Charlotte Street, just above Dorchester and found the address Burtya had given me. It proved to be an old brick house at street level with a yard behind it, a lane on one side and an apartment building on the other. I went in and asked for old Demitro.

"He's in the cathouse next door," Charlie's wife told me. "We didn't have a spare room for him here so Charlie had to get him a room in the whorehouse. He's got a nice clean room in the basement."

I looked at the woman and I remembered what I had heard about her. No wonder she looked so haggard. Never enough money, too many screaming brats and nothing but abuse from the neighbours, her husband, the cops, and even the other Gypsy women, because she wasn't a born Gypsy. Gypsy women pick on the outsider who has married one of their men. Bonnie was obviously suffering from acute malnutrition. I wondered if this was what Marie would be like one day. I looked at the wedding photo on the wall, near the family shrine and saw that Bonnie, too, had once been beautiful, a waitress who'd fallen in love with a Gypsy bum in a hash house in Halifax.

I went next door to look for the old man's room. The building consisted of one-room apartments. I went down the cellar staircase and came to a doorway frame with drapes and a gauze curtain in lieu of a door. It was a typical Gypsy-looking setup designed to lure in clients for a palm reading. But the old man didn't tell fortunes, I realized as I entered and saw the mistake I'd made. A plump prostitute was sitting on a high stool in front of a large vanity with a huge mirror, combing her long black hair. I saw the crucifix on the wall underneath the ornate picture of the Savior and realized that she was a practising Roman Catholic. All she had on were a pair of net stockings, a black garter belt and a scanty brassiere. She saw me in the mirror and turned around on the swivel stool to face me, flashing the black hair of her pussy as she lifted one plump thigh.

"*Quinze piastres*," she told me, "fifteen bucks."

"Sorry," I replied in French. "I was looking for the old Gypsy man. I must be in the wrong room."

She got up, came over to me, grabbed my hand and pulled me over to the large bed where she sat down holding my right hand with her left.

"I give you a nice jig-a-jig, Gypsy boy," she told me, opening my zipper with her right hand and pulling out my whacker.

"*Et je te suce la graine aussi poour cinq piastres de plus,*" she added.

"*Non, merci,*" I said, as she took my pecker in her hand and pouted her sexy red lips to show me what she meant. "*Non, merci, mademoiselle, vous êtes belle mais je n'ai pas d'argent. Une autre fois, peut-être.*"

"No money," she screamed. "Get out before I call the police."

I left in a hurry, stuffing my weapon back inside my trousers and pulling up my zipper. I tried the next door, and this time I knocked to make sure it was the old man's room.

I found him sitting on his bed, fully dressed, even to his hat. Like all Gypsies of his generation he was always fully dressed indoors. They were used to living in tents, wagons and trailers. He looked both sad and regal sitting there, all dressed up and nowhere to go. There was a large, wet stain on the ceiling; water was dripping onto his floor and he had thrown some newspapers and rags to soak it up. The water made a steady plop, plop, as it hit the paper. A defective toilet upstairs? His homemade crest was hanging from his left shirt pocket, his *pechata*, or badge of leadership, the emblem of the patriarch. I saw his shrine and holy icons on the wall and the picture of Jesus Christ hanging over his cracked enamel sink. He smiled when he saw me and I asked his permission to wash my hands in his sink before I shook hands with him. I'd just handled my whacker and would have defiled him if I hadn't cleansed my hands.

"Sit down, Yanko," he told me. "I knew you'd come when you heard I was back."

The years were catching up, but he was still alert and active, though just past seventy. It was five years since he'd married Marie and me in Kolia's old house on St. Urbain Street.

"I'll make you some tea," he said as he got up and turned on the gas range, placing his ancient copper kettle on the stove.

I heard some violent sounds coming from just across the hallway.

"What's going on out there?" I asked him.

"Oh, that's one of the men working in the parking lot across the street," he told me. "He comes here and pays the women to beat him up now and again. He's sadistic." Demitro called all unconventional sex "sadistic".

We drank our tea as the sounds subsided and a small man came out of the room across the hall, saw us through the open door and came in.

"I wanted to see you, Demitro," he told the old man. "Tell your Gypsy boys to stop putting their stinking cars on the lot. Every time one of the fucking customers wants to park there, there's no stinking room. What the hell do you Gypsies do with so many cars, anyway?"

"We sell them," Demitro smiled pleasantly. "But my people pay for whatever space they take. What's the trouble?"

"I know they pay," the man agreed. "But a lot of syndicate boys go to the gambling casino up the street. Those hoods get mad like hell when there's no place for them. The cops are tough around here on parking violations and the women in here are complaining too. Their johns got no place to park either. Christ, Demitro, the price of ass is high enough these days without finding a ticket on your car as well when you get out. It's bad for business all around. You'll have to find somewhere else for those Gypsy cars."

"I'll tell them," the old man said without rancour. It was his duty as a patriarch of Canada's Gypsies to keep the hoodlums, the whores and the Gypsies living in harmony in the slums. I wondered, absently, just how well some of our gifted Canadian statesmen would handle this situation.

"How is Mara and your children?" Demitro asked me after the man left. "How many do you have now?"

"Marie's fine," I told him. "I have two daughters now, and another baby on the way."

"It's good to have a large family," he said. "I had nine sons and six daughters, but one died, poor little Rosie."

He glanced at the faded brown daguerreotype on the wall.

"She died in South Carolina," he went on, "and they buried her there, in the black people's cemetery."

A young Gypsy boy about nine came into the room.

"Dad wants to see you next door right away," he told the old man.

We went next door and found Charlie sitting at his living room table with two non-Gypsies. There was a pile of rings, watches, and other junk lying on the table in front of them. Charlie had taken off his shirt; his underwear top was yellow and dirty. He was about forty-five, fattish and had lost almost all his hair. He motioned towards the pile of stuff.

"*So gindis, Mo?*" he said. "What do you figure, Dad?"

The old man sat down and went through the pile as I sat on the couch nearby. He rejected most of the stuff and made a smaller pile to one side. He had a lifetime of buying and selling everything from horses to wedding rings, and now his experience was invaluable to his son.

I looked at Charlie's little boy standing nearby watching them, and saw the three generations and the gradual Canadianization of my people. The old man had been an honest dealer, his son was a fence, what about his grandson? Would he end up a thief like those two Canadian crooks sitting there with his father? The old man turned to his son.

"*Panshwardesh dileri,*" he said.

"Fifty smackers for the bunch," Charlie translated for the hoods.

"It's worth at least a hundred," Paddy, the bigger of the two men, said. He was a heavy-set guy with a cherub-like expression and a mop of greyish hair. He looked like a church minister in his black tropical suit and grey straw hat. His partner was shorter, younger and darker, and used the name "Giovanni".

"Oh, what's the use?" Giovanni argued. "We take what they give us and steal some more stuff. Where else are we gonna get rid of this junk?"

They accepted the fifty dollars and put the unwanted loot back inside their leatherette briefcases. They might be hustlers and thieves, but they didn't commit crimes of violence.

"You guys want a beer?" Charlie asked them.

"Sure," Paddy replied. "We like to be sociable."

Bonnie went to the fridge and brought us all beers.

"Where'd you get the loot?" Paddy asked Charlie as he saw shelves full of beer.

"Welfare cheque just came through," Charlie explained. "I got a good disability, a hernia, and my war pension too, I was wounded."

In truth, Charlie had been drafted into the Canadian Home Defense Force during World War II. The jeep he'd been driving for three officers had overturned on the icy highway on the way back from a private party and Charlie had injured his spine. He would be on public welfare for the rest of his life. His hernia had been caused by helping Paddy and Giovanni unload stolen television sets from a panel truck. His sideline, as a fence, provided him with extra money for drink, the horses and women. Charlie hadn't always been like this, but the blow he got on the head from a pipe wrench a few years ago when Burtya sent some hired thugs to run him out of town hadn't helped his intellectual abilities.

"Yeah, his welfare cheque," Bonnie yelled back from the stove where she was cooking. "He lost most of it on the nags yesterday and now he's guzzling the rest. God distorted him and flung him to me." She added a curse in Romani, which she spoke as well as any Gypsy.

We drank our beer as the old man outlined his plan to form a Gypsy representation committee. "We have to get organized and approach the Government before it's too late," he told us, as I watched a bedbug emerge from under his collar and walk across the white shirt, onto his dark grey suit.

"Gypsies aren't born criminals," he went on. "But now we're forced to break the law to feed our families."

"We all gotta break the law to eat," Paddy interrupted, "and we ain't even Gypsies."

"We have to form a group of responsible Gypsy elders," Demitro said, "and approach the Government to make them aware of the problem. In the old days we worked the carnivals, travelled all over North America making our living honestly. We had merry-go-rounds, stalls, we bought and sold things and our women told fortunes, but then the big combines bought up the carnival rights and forced us out. We tried the small-time outfits but even that's finished now with television and new laws. All these permits and licences and new bylaws. People were more human in the old days, they used to live and let live, now they want to have a monopoly on everything. The authorities keep passing new laws to stop us doing the things we can still do like selling from door to door, operating stands on the street corner and all we have left now is the used car business and illegal fortunetelling. If one of Burtya's women steals, they refuse to give licences to any Gypsy regardless of whether they steal or not. Only a few of our women are thieves, you know that."

I nodded. "They should arrest only the guilty women and leave the others alone to make an honest living. What the hell's wrong with fortunetelling? Gypsies tell fortunes in the States, in England, South America and Europe; nobody bothers them, even in Communist countries. Why can't they do it here in Canada?"

"The church," Paddy butted in. "That's their monopoly in Quebec."

"How many are interested?" I asked the old man.

"Well," he began, "about a dozen or so of the older men, and you and I, of course."

I noticed that he'd left out all of his own sons, but said nothing. I glanced out through the open window facing onto the street and saw a uniformed policeman looking in at us with obvious interest. I turned to Paddy, my face showing alarm.

"He's O.K.," Paddy smiled, "a thief like us."

"The first thing I'd like to do," the old man continued, more for my benefit this time, "is to put down our language on paper. I want to make a dictionary of Romani. If we can prove that we have a language all of our own, people will know that we're different. I'll tell you all the words, Yanko, and you can write them down with your typewriter. Then we'll take them to Isaac Pitman in Toronto and he'll publish them for us. He's a fine gentleman, Mr. Pitman, I met him years ago when my wife was alive and telling fortunes. He said there was no such thing as a dictionary of Romani. But that's not really true. A *Gazho* once tried to make a dictionary of Romani. I have it upstairs in my trunk if you'd like to look at it. It's not very good; that's why I want to do a better one."

I told him I'd like very much to see it. I was intrigued. What had this old man stumbled on in his travels, Paspati, Sampson, Lelland, Borrow, what?

We climbed the stairs to Charlie's attic where the old man kept his *lada*, his travelling trunk, not unlike a typical treasure chest from a pirate movie. It was very old. He opened it, rummaged through it and finally produced a small, blue-coloured booklet which he handed to me.

It had been written years before by a police department in the southern United States. It had a list of about fifty words of Romani, badly transcribed and many with the wrong translation. It was a training manual for candidates for the force and it gave a brief description of the types of rackets and swindles likely to be attempted by Gypsies and other carnival types in their gambling games and other concessions. It was one of the old man's most treasured possessions.

"We can certainly do better than that," I assured him.

— 11 —

Next morning I got up early and decided to let my peddling go for the day. I'd explained the old man's plan to Marie the evening before, and now I wanted to get some good publicity for him. Marie didn't share my enthusiasm.

"What the hell did they ever do for my people?" she told me. "We've been telling these fools for years what we want, what we need. But they still treat us like dumb savages and figure the only way they can help us is to make good Christian white people out of us. You Gypsies are better off the way you are. As soon as the Government gets after you, you'll end up on reservations in shacks with a wooden shithouse outside."

"You're too bitter," I argued.

"You'll find out, tenderfoot," she told me. "But you'd better wear an earring and take Jilko's fiddle with you, otherwise they might not believe you're a Gypsy."

I called George, a journalist friend of mine who was freelance, and asked him how to go about getting some good publicity for the old man. He advised me to contact a magazine called *Canadian Ethnic Culture* that was always looking for stories of this type.

"Great," I told him. "Just what we need. They'll send a reporter who has experience in reporting from the minority viewpoint."

I telephoned a Miss Percival and she agreed to come to my apartment. She would interview me, then go down to see the old man. I phoned Charlie and told him to install his father in his house like he was living there.

"Fix up the place a bit," I added, "and for Christ's sake keep those two burglars out while the old man is being interviewed."

"Will do," Charlie agreed.

Jilko had lunch with us. He was out of work again. We talked and played with Delilah and Helen, my two baby girls. They kept trying to pick Jilko's pocket. I wondered where they'd learned that. Probably at the Gypsy feasts and other gatherings. It was a game among the Gypsy girls. Miss Percival finally arrived about three o'clock along with a sad-eyed Greek freelance photographer called Pavlos. Miss Percival was an English-Canadian reporter, poorly educated, dull-witted and very plainly dressed. She had the photographer take a few shots of Marie wearing the traditional Gypsy costume.

"A typical Gypsy woman," she told me. "I've seen them in Spain."

Then she had some shots taken of my ship models, fifteen in all, the basis of a collection showing the history and gradual evolution of the ship from the earliest Nile boats of the Egyptians through classical times to the Middle Ages, finally culminating in my clipper ship, *Flying Cloud*.

"Why don't you sell these little boats?" she asked me, after I'd explained that I couldn't get a decent job and was existing by selling junk imports.

"Nobody wants them," I said. "Each takes months of research and work."

I pointed to the orange crates full of books and loose leaf note-books along the wall.

"People don't seem to realize the work it takes to build an accurate replica. They offer me ten dollars or so."

"You should move to the Maritimes," she advised me. "Open a souvenir stand. That's where people go to look for knickknacks like these."

But the Greek photographer was thrilled by my collection. "These belong in a museum," he told me. "They're as good as anything I've seen in Europe."

Miss Percival seemed disappointed when I told her that Gypsy men in Canada had no colourful or distinctive costume of their own.

I then got into Miss Percival's small English-made car with her and Pavlos and we drove over to Charlie's place. On the way she asked me another pointed question.

"Mr. Lee, is it true that Gypsy children are taught to pick pockets by their parents by practising on a dummy rigged up with bells and if they can't get the wallet out of the dummy's pocket without ringing the bells they don't get any supper?"

I laughed. "Maybe in Arabia or some country where people are shrewd and wide awake. But the dummies in Canada who are stupid enough to go into Gypsy mitt joints are either so stoned on liquor or so eager to get their expected sex that you could probably saw one of their legs off and they wouldn't know it until after they got back out of the store. You don't need any methods that sophisticated in this country. It's funny," I added, "how people always put their own vices onto the Gypsies. In Hungary they say 'she makes love like a Gypsy' or in Yugoslavia 'he drinks like a Gypsy'. Why are Anglo-Saxons so obsessed with Gypsy theft, even the word gyp. 'He tried to gyp me but I jewed him down,' isn't that a typical English-Canadian expression?"

She didn't answer that one. When we arrived I found that Bonnie had fixed up the place as best she could. Charlie was wearing a new shirt, sports jacket, non-functional tie clip and new shoes, probably some stuff his friends had brought around.

I introduced everybody and Miss Percival set up her tape recorder as Pavlos started taking shots of the house inside and out.

"I hope they won't put those pictures in the papers," Bonnie told me in Romani. "We might lose our welfare benefits if they find out we're Gypsies."

Miss Percival seemed to understand.

"We only want you and Mister Demitro," she told me. "I won't mention the others."

"Will you have to give the address or location?" I asked.

She smiled demurely. "Not really."

Then she went into action by asking the old man questions on tape.

The old man talked to her like he was talking to another Gypsy. He told her about the women who stole and about how the police arrested them for prostitution when the actual crime was that of lifting a few bucks from some drunk's wallet or, more often, simply for telling fortunes illegally. He tried honestly to present his case to a rational human being.

Suddenly Paddy and Giovanni appeared in front of the store and motioned to Charlie who got up, excused himself and left. I saw the three of them heading for the whorehouse next door, I presumed to go to the old man's room to do business.

"Charlie went out to sell his car to a couple of friends," I told

Miss Percival as she went on to ask the old man about the past, the horses, the tents, the wagons, violins and all the other trappings of the pseudo-Gypsy culture she'd read about.

Charlie returned with an expensive-looking watch and showed it to his father. "Twenty like this," he said in Romani.

The old man studied the watch, oblivious to the reporter.

"Five dollars each," he replied, also in Romani.

Charlie left.

"What was all that about?" Miss Percival asked.

"Charlie's friends offered him the watch as part payment for the car," I lied. "He's looking for a job and he needs a watch badly so he can be on time for his appointments."

Thank God he hadn't been wearing a watch when he came in. He was always selling the one he had to buy booze. Why not? He'd soon have a few more.

Miss Percival went on with the interview as I lit a cigarette. Then I heard Charlie in the doorway arguing with the two hoods. He came in alone swearing in Romani as the hoods passed the window.

"*Mek len te han muro kar*," he snarled.

"What did he say?" Miss Percival asked.

"I just sold the car," I told her.

"I thought the last word was 'car'," she said. "You see, I'm already learning your language."

What Charlie had really said was, "Let them eat my prick." *Kar*, in Romani, means penis. She wrote down the sentence as I dictated it to her, word for word.

Now, another interruption. Some character the old man had once met while in the hospital came in. He was a mysterious looking guy, well educated and well off, a psychiatrist or something. He had started to visit the Gypsies, jotting down words of Romani, attending weddings and feasts and collecting bits of folklore. In England he would have been called a Gypsiologist but the term had no meaning in Canada. He was also a good customer of Charlie's.

I followed as Charlie took him into the back of the house, placed an expensive record player on the table and put a record on the turntable. He then worked all the gimmicks and gadgets to show that it was operating smoothly and the man slipped Charlie some money as Bonnie wrapped up the player in brown paper and tied a string around it. The Gypsiologist then left by Charlie's back door, carrying his prize under his arm heading for the alleyway, from which he could emerge next to the casino on St. Catherine Street where anybody seeing him would assume that he was coming from the bootlegger and pay no attention.

"Who was that?" Miss Percival asked.

"Charlie fixed his record player," I explained.

"Versatile man, isn't he?" she said, looking at Charlie. "He won't have much trouble finding a good job in a city as big as Montreal."

"No, he won't," I assured her. "There's always lots of openings for his particular talents and abilities. He's never unemployed for long."

She asked the old man to tell her about Gypsy life as he'd known it back in his younger days.

"Things were different then," the old man began. "My people came from the old country, Serbia, and we travelled all over America. I was born somewhere in the South. At first we kept to ourselves, travelling like we used to, trading horses and mules, selling things to the farmers and doing repairs to equipment and kitchen utensils. Then we joined the carnivals and circuses."

"Can you tell me something about the carnivals for our readers?" Miss Percival asked. "Some anecdote that you think would interest them. How did you live then, did you have money?"

"Of course we had money," the old man told her, "gold. I remember one time we were travelling across Canada with a carnival train. Mostly *Gazhe* but a few Gypsy families, and we ran out of funds near Edmonton. The carnival operators wanted to disband the train right there, but I loaned them enough to keep going until we got to Fort William where we made a killing. But then in the twenties the American government wanted all the gold, they paid cash for it and most of our people sold their gold for money. Then they bought big cars and trailers and spent the rest on feasts and fancy clothes. Soon they had no money and no gold. Then the carnivals folded and we had to move into the cities. That was the end of the old life. Now the young Gypsies born in the cities don't know the old life and they haven't got the education of the *Gazhe* to get good jobs."

"But surely," Miss Percival argued, "Gypsies can be educated. If your children went to school they'd have the same advantages as any other child."

I looked at her. "I'm educated and I'm here, so is my wife.

Demitro himself is literate. It's not a matter of education, my friend, it's a little thing called prejudice and fear of the unknown. Gypsies will assimilate eventually, like any other minority, by way of the slums, vice, the destruction of their culture and self-respect, but not as Gypsies. The Gypsy by his very existence is the negation of all the hypocritical values that society holds dear. He can't be allowed to exist as is, he has to be lobotomized like any other savage or nigger before he can enter the white man's world."

"But the world is changing." Miss Percival argued. "The young generation is abandoning the old prejudices and values. They're looking for new values, this is an age of change."

I smiled. "So was Babylon, Rome and all the other decadent civilizations. Nothing new is happening, believe me, the cycle is only repeating itself. There were hippies in Egypt before it fell."

"What do you think?" she asked Demitro.

He smiled gently. "*Sap bianel sap,*" he replied, "A snake always bears a snake."

She finally got through with the interview. I hoped she would get out before some other local hoodlum walked in. Of all the places to hold an interview it had to be in the home of the only Gypsy fence in Canada. The other Gypsies wouldn't deal in the stuff at all, but Charlie had to make all the money in the family; his wife wasn't a Gypsy and couldn't tell fortunes. Well-meaning English-Canadians were always telling me that part of the problem confronting my people was their stubborn refusal to intermarry with Canadians of other origins. Christ, I thought, there might be an army of Gypsy fences from Halifax to Vancouver if more Gypsy men had married non-Gypsy women.

Miss Percival started packing her gear into a leather carry-all and I handed her a typewritten report.

"This is something I wrote about the Gypsies in Canada," I told her.

She stuffed it into her bag and I went out to stand in the doorway and get some fresh air.

"What is that guy in there, a fence?"

It was Pavlos, the Greek.

"Could be, *Cubaros,*" I said. "But what's it to you? You're not a reporter or a cop."

"No," he said pleasantly. "But I need equipment, cameras, lights, stuff like that. I want to open my own studio instead of being forced to work for peanuts for these exploiting English-Canadian pigs."

"O.K. *philosmu,*" I told him. "Stick around after that moron leaves and I'll introduce you to the boys. I know your problem."

I liked the Greek instinctively. We had similar vibrations and I felt that he was having a similar struggle and a similar rejection.

Miss Percival came out of Charlie's joint and thanked me profusely for helping her. She assured me that she would do a good story.

"Try to get them to use a good headline," I told her.

"Word of honor," she replied.

What the hell did that mean? I wondered.

She drove off as Paddy and Giovanni returned with more stuff. We all went back inside the house. Now that the establishment was gone, things were back to normal.

"What's that Greek doing here?" Charlie asked me in Romani.

"He's O.K.," I replied in English. "He wants to buy some good cameras cheap, maybe the boys can help him."

"Sit down, *Cubaros,*" Charlie smiled paternally. A lot of his best customers were Greeks.

"What are you looking for, buddy?" Paddy asked Pavlos.

The Greek told him.

"Will do," Paddy smiled. "Stolen to order, that's my line."

Like my old friend Alec would have said, "Simplicity, man, simplicity. Why steal something nobody wants."

Pavlos and I then took the old man back to his room in the brothel and he asked me to drop around the following night to start work on the dictionary.

"I'm getting old," he said simply.

The Greek was horrified when he saw where old Demitro was living.

"Terrible," he said. "A fine old man like that having to end his days living in the basement of a house of prostitution."

"That's progress, Pavlos," I told him. "The skyscrapers go up and the Gypsies go down."

"Let's go have a drink," Pavlos suggested.

We went to a nearby Greek social club on St. Lawrence Boulevard, the hangout of Greek immigrants, where the orchestra made with Greek music. A beautiful girl came onto the stage wearing an

Arabian belly dancer's outfit and did her thing, twirling in somersaults to the oriental music of the band. She had bells and cymbals on her feet and fingers and I could hardly believe that I was still in Canada. She finished her dance and left the stage. I noticed a group of men sitting at one of the tables, obvious gangsters. The dancer joined them, they talked for a while, then she left in a hurry, seemingly annoyed. The gangsters also left and Pavlos got onto the stage and did a couple of Greek dances, throwing money onto the floor in front of the orchestra as was the Greek custom.

Later, we decided to leave; neither of us had much money. We walked down the narrow stairs to find a crowd of people gathered around a small figure lying in the street outside. It was the oriental dancer. As we went closer I heard her moaning in Greek, delirious with pain. Pavlos knelt over her as the police arrived. The two cops pushed their way through the crowd, chased Pavlos away from the girl and covered her with a horse blanket to wait for the ambulance.

"What happened?" I asked Pavlos.

"Those men in the club," he told me. "They had somebody break her legs with a crowbar when she came out."

"Anybody see what happened?" a cop asked in French.

Nobody spoke.

"I can identify those guys," Pavlos said to me. "I have them on film. I take snapshots of the customers in these Greek clubs on the weekends."

He opened his mouth to call to the policeman as I grabbed his arm.

"Listen, you idiot," I told him. "Stay out of it unless you want to end up in the St. Lawrence with a pair of cement shoes along with the girl. Nobody can touch those guys, they're in *La Pègre*, they're beyond the law."

12

It was finally here, the day the article was to appear. We waited two months to see it and it was due on the newstands this morning. I left early while Marie was still sleeping. After I bought the magazine, I decided I needed a drink, and from here that meant the Bistro on Mountain Street. I took a good slug of my beer, opened the magazine and looked at the headline:

"*Canada's Gypsy King Defends Criminal Subjects From Montreal Headquarters...*"

It described the old man as "king" of Canada's nomads and the old upholstered chair that Charlie had picked up from the Salvation Army depot as his throne. It went on to describe Charlie the fence as a "jack of all trades" and me as the talented young Gypsy who made beautiful little boats. I was glad that very few of the Gypsies could read. It did say that some of the women picked pockets, but failed to mention that the police then arrested them for prostitution. It also included statements from numerous police officials as far away as Vancouver describing Gypsy crime. It had a lot to say about the Gypsies in Spain and Czechoslovakia, but it included nothing from the detailed report I had given her.

"Hi Yanko," a voice boomed across the table.

I looked up and saw Bill Murphy, another Montrealer like myself. We'd grown up together in the same slums.

"Nice story," he said. "You masochist."

"No good?" I asked him.

"Crap," he said. "Real crap."

Bill was a man of the revolution. He had a lucid mind and had read extensively. His pet theme was political reform in Canada. He was an English-Canadian and couldn't retreat into the defence of an ethnic minority group that was being victimized, like me and most of our mutual friends who were Indians, Blacks, French-Canadians or some other sub-human Canadian element. To Bill the whole thing was political. The system had to go. He'd been all for the N.D.P., like the rest of us, until he saw that they too were just part of our political fantasia and were just playing ring around the rosy like the two major parties. "John gets up, Lester sits down and Tommy's too small to get in the game. Thief and Faker, Smearson and Bugger us, the musical chair boys, nothing ever changes and the music goes on forever."

That, in a nutshell, was his analysis of Canadian politics. Later, he was all for Pretty Pierre whom he now called "Turdeau."

"Pigs, that's what they are," he said as he sat down.

"Two beers," he yelled to a passing waiter. "You shouldn't have got mixed up with those idiots, Yanko."

George who had put me onto Miss Percival, came in and joined us. He thought the article was quite good.

"You see, Yanko," he explained, "when you write in Canada, you gotta write for the average Joe with egg on his chin and brown stains on his underwear. Not deep, creative stuff, but down-to-earth Canadian humour, like you were talking to a truckdriver in the shithouse of a tavern."

"I suppose so," I said.

"What are you doing for a living now, anyway?" George asked.

"Not much," I told him. "I had to give up that Hindu imported stuff, now that the Japanese imitations of it are flooding the department stores. I've gone back to doing piece work for second hand junk dealers and mail order houses, fixing movie projectors, typewriters, tape recorders and other stuff. I make around fifty bucks or so in a good week."

"How can you live on that?" he asked.

"We manage," I told him.

"Still building your little boats?" he asked.

"Yes," I said, tiredly. "I'm still making my little boats. I've got sixteen of them now, red ones, yellow ones and black ones."

"Why don't you try the Canada Council," he suggested. "Apply for a grant."

I looked at him, bored. "I already have, but ship-model building doesn't come under their definition of art. You have to be something obvious like the town fool of Vancouver. I'm not eligible."

"What about Expo?" he said.

"Christ, George," I told him. "I've wasted enough time with those dummies already. They claim they don't need me, if they want anything maritime they figure they can get it easily from the Maritimes."

"Well, can't they?" he argued. "I mean, after all, you'd think that if they want something maritime they should be able to get it from the Maritimes, I mean, it's logical."

"Sure, it's logical," I told him. "This country is so fucking logical it's become highly illogical. Who needs the years of research and experience I've built up, studying and making models when you've got an army of semi-literate woodcarvers down there. Any axe-wielding fisherman can build a replica of a Byzantine dromond at a scale of eight feet to the inch."

"I've got a good job lined up," he told me. "In publicity, a hundred and eighty bucks a week plus expenses, car allowance, everything."

I got fed up listening and left for the old man's place. I found him fully dressed in his room busy reading a copy of the article. There was quite a commotion in the whorehouse, a prostitute had been murdered the night before.

"It's not too bad," the old man said getting up to make me some tea, but I knew he was hurt. You can call a Gypsy a thief, a pig, and he will laugh in your face. But if he slips on the ice and breaks the bottle of milk he's carrying and somebody laughs, look out. The one thing he can't stand is to be ridiculed. He told me about the murdered whore.

"Tied her up, gagged her and burned her with cigarettes, then he stabbed her to death. What kind of a man would do a terrible thing like that? God made whores just like he made everybody else; it stops men from bothering honest women. It must have been one of those crazy Frenchmen," he concluded. "I knew of a Frenchmen once, in New Orleans. He strangled five women before they finally shot him."

"Who's paying the rent for this room?" I asked. I was getting fed up seeing him living here in this brothel.

"I am," he told me. "Fifty-five dollars a month. My pension is only sixty but I make some extra money by selling things to the women here for Paddy and Giovanni. But they want to throw me out, the women are after this room. They can get a hundred dollars a month from the *kurvi*."

"How would you like to live with Marie, Jilko and me?" I asked him.

His old eyes shone as he looked at me.

"I wouldn't be any trouble," he told me. "I can still look after myself, go to the bathroom and everything."

I'd have to get the others to agree, but I knew we could work out something if we all chipped in and rented a large old house.

Suddenly Marie appeared in the doorway, very excited.

"Jilko's just been arrested. One of the Hungarian Gypsies came and told me. Jilko says for you to go and see him right away, he's in Number One."

I sent Marie home with Paddy who was just leaving Charlie's place, then went over to the police station with the old man. They knew him well. He waited downstairs while I went up to see Jilko. I was allowed to speak to him through a small opening covered with wire mesh.

"What happened?" I asked him.

"I steal," he said simply. "Police is catch me."

He'd gone to the bank to draw out his last few dollars and he'd seen some old lady take an enormous sum of money from the teller. He'd tried to grab her purse and run for it but some hefty customers had grabbed him and he'd stabbed one of them with his pocket knife in the resulting melée.

"Why did you do it?" I asked.

"I sick here, Yanko," he said sadly. "Dis country not good for Hungarian Gypsy people. Nobody is vant Gypsy music. I got no job, no money, no woman, nothing. And everybody is call me D.P. I vant to take money and go back to Hungary. Communists is not so bad," he went on. "I still can play violin and make good money to drink and have plenty *rakli* (girls). I no open mouth, not say anything against Communists, is nobody bother me. I live with Gypsy people and play Gypsy music. Vat happen now, Yanko?"

"I'll go and see the Gypsy lawyer," I told him.

I left Jilko and went back to the old man.

"These young Gypsies are crazy," he said. "When I was young we never stole anything but chickens. Nowadays, the Gypsies take all kinds of chances, they've gone mad."

"No, Uncle," I argued. "The world's gone mad!'

We found the Gypsy lawyer in his office in the slums near the Main. He ushered us into his inner office, dismissed his secretary and shut the door. He was a porcine-looking man with heavy jowls and a worried-looking face.

"What is it this time, Demitro?" he asked the old man.

"A young Gypsy friend of mine just got arrested for attempted theft," I told him.

"Oh, Jesus Christ." He sounded disgusted. "So what happened, any witnesses, violence, fatalities?"

I explained all I knew about the case.

"Not much I can do," he said. "I'll go see the punk though. Maybe I can get the charge reduced to temporary insanity. No chance I can expect to get paid anything for this, I suppose."

"I can give you something," I said. "A few dollars a week."

"You're a deadbeat, Yanko," he told me. "You can hardly support yourself and your squaw. I guess I'll just have to be magnanimous again."

I took the old man home. As we walked down Berger and onto Charlotte we saw Charlie ahead of us, staggering and weaving his way along the street holding onto the walls, accompanied by the cacophony of the clanging garbage cans and the sound of the crusher as the garbage truck followed him and the men emptied the bins. He reached his home ahead of us, managed to ring the bell, then fell in the street beside the garbage can. Bonnie opened the door and looked at him just as we caught up. Then she turned and yelled at the garbage collector who was carrying away the family trash can: "Hey you, you forgot something. Take him away as well while you're at it."

We got Charlie to his feet and inside the house where Bonnie had us put him on the bed, then we left and went to the whorehouse next door.

"Poor Charlie," the old man said, shaking his head, "must have got his relief cheque this morning and gone to the tavern to cash it. I don't understand these young Gypsies. When I was his age we only drank at feasts and weddings, we never went to the taverns like the *Gazhe*."

"That's the Canadian melting pot," I told him, "the tavern. Ethnic differences disappear when you're all drunk."

When I got home Marie brought me a plate of beans. She'd read

113

the article by now and she kept glancing at the magazine lying on the couch nearby as I ate.

"All right," I told her, "you were right."

"What are you going to do now?" she asked.

I showed her a press clipping I'd been saving for weeks mulling over it. It was a report on how the Gypsies in Europe had organized themselves into a solid group to bring the attention of the outside world to the problems confronting the Romani people in the twentieth century. They were campaigning internationally for representation in the United Nations, self-determination and international identity as a people in their own right. These were educated Gypsies with a headquarters in Paris, The World Romani Community. She read it.

"I'm going to volunteer to represent my people in Canada," I told her. "If they accept me I'll show the bastards what it means to make fun of an old man."

She looked at me, a bit sadly.

"You'll learn someday, Yanko," she said. "But go ahead. Just remember that the Indians always lose in the end."

She went back into the kitchen to make the kids some supper and I realized that she would soon be having another baby. Christ, I thought, when the hell would they allow the pill in this cesspool of a theocracy.

I went onto the gallery outside my workshop to sit in the old deckchair, watching my two little girls playing beside me. They smiled and climbed all over me, happy to see me. I drank the beer Marie brought me, relaxed and watched the men working on the underpass on Park Avenue below Pine. Wouldn't they ever get through with that project? The pneumatic drills had been going ever since we moved in here almost five years ago and the dust was always getting into the house and all over my ship models.

A flashy American car with Illinois plates drove up the street and stopped in front of my place. A man got out, glanced up at the gallery and I recognized Kolia.

"Kolia," I yelled at him in Romani. "God has sent you."

I went through my studio at the top of the stairs and pulled the rope to open the door below. He rushed up the stairs, shouting and laughing as Marie came to see what all the commotion was about.

Kolia looked older, more worried. He'd lost that European Gypsy look he used to have.

114

"Where are the old people and Tinka?" I asked him.

"My father died in Chicago," he told me, "my mother is with some distant relatives of mine in Hull. I left Tinka just after my father died. I'm alone again."

"How's your work going?" I asked.

"It's bad, Yanko," he told me. "They're bringing in stainless steel basins now, they don't need to be plated. All I'm doing now is restaurants, but the big companies are moving into this with low paid immigrant labour. I can't make the money I used to."

He called up the supermarket and had some food and beer delivered. As we drank, I told him about the old man's dream.

"He's crazy," Kolia said. "A lot of Gypsies tried that in Europe, they're all dead. In a free country Gypsies don't need representation committees."

I put a Flamenco record on the old record player. Kolia liked this Spanish Gypsy music, it reminded him of his former life in Spain. He told me of the great parties and feasts his people used to have there, then got up and did a clumsy imitation of a Flamenco dancer. The Coppersmith Gypsies don't have the agility and grace of the Spanish Gitanos.

"*Olé*," he shouted, almost slipping in his new American shoes, "*Olé, como la raza Cale.*"

Marie smiled at me and squeezed my hand, remembering the past. I felt happy that Kolia had returned. At least now I would have someone to work with.

13

Next day, I went with Kolia to Hull where we picked up his mother and brought her back to Montreal. We took over a large old house on de Bullion Street and old Demitro moved in with us.

A little while later, I received my identity card from the World Romani Community as the delegate general in Canada; the old man represented his people; together we hoped to do something constructive. We opened an office in the front room where the old man slept, and hung the blue and green flag of the Romani people on the wall.

The money problems eased somewhat now that I was working with Kolia again. We bought some decent furniture and fixed up the place as best we could. This was the first real home Marie and I had had since we were married. The old house had been a whorehouse during the war years, as had many of the houses on infamous de Bullion Street. The scrawled obscenities and *graffiti* were still to be seen on the wallpaper in places.

Kolia would go off by himself to look for work while his mother stayed with us. He would line up a few jobs, then come back for me and we would leave for a few days to do the work. I feared the coming winter when the roads would become impassable and we would have to rely on work in the city. It wasn't easy now to get jobs locally. I had launched my press campaign and there were numerous stories and taped interviews on me as the Canadian delegate of the World Romani Community.

Today was Sunday and I had another interview coming up with a woman freelancer who did taped radio shows on various topics of interest. Marie as usual, wasn't overly enthusiastic.

"Go if you want," she told me. "But it's probably just some horny old bag who wants to meet you."

The old man was more enthusiastic.

"Tell her about our dictionary," he suggested.

Kolia had helped a lot, he would sit for hours with the old man and me as I went over the lists of words. One thing the old man couldn't seem to understand was the fact that I first had to speak the language as well as he did in order to compile the dictionary. I couldn't just write down words that he dictated to me. I had to get living examples of the language to analyze from him or from Kolia. Kolia would sit watching, then on the spur of the moment, he might suddenly ask me, "Yanko, do you have *priboi*?"

"What's that?" I'd ask.

"Centre-punch," he'd tell me in French, Spanish or some other language. His English was still limited.

"No, I haven't," I'd tell him, then go through the basic word groupings and place the word where it belonged. Often, the old man would offer another term having the same meaning. Neither word was original Romani but had been picked up from other languages in the countries where the Gypsies had lived. Romani was studded with these borrowed terms and each particular dialect had a different group although the standard Romani words and grammar were all of Indic origin.

"Yanko," Kolia would then exclaim, looking at me with reverence, almost with awe. "How do you know which words you haven't got?"

Today, I had risen early. It was the beginning of autumn and the old man had gone down to Charlie's place. Some Gypsies had arrived in town from Hamilton and Charlie was giving a *pakiv*, or feast, in their honour.

I went downtown and found that the woman journalist was living in a large, luxurious high-rise apartment building. She had a penthouse and I got a splendid view of the city from where I sat. She joined me and set up her tape recorder. She wore a silk Japanese housecoat and I could see through it to her brassiere, panties and stockings underneath. She was about forty-five and obviously went to the beauty parlour regularly. The only other occupant of the place was her poodle, now lying fast asleep on the rug near the nude statue of Apollo.

She brought me a beer and herself a glass of whisky, which she placed on the small coffee table in front of me. Then she sat on a footstool beside me and the housecoat opened enough to give me a good view of her thighs and their varicose veins. Marie needn't have worried. She was much too old and withered.

"I really enjoy these informal interviews," she told me. "It's much cozier than doing things down in the C.B.C. building."

She handed me some papers. "I've outlined the type of questions I'd like to ask you, if you'd care to look through this. You do read, don't you?"

"Most of my people are illiterate," I told her, "but I'm not, nor is the old man, Demitro."

We finished our drinks as I examined the papers. She'd planned a "women only" type interview, all the questions were about domestic affairs among the Gypsies, but I managed at the end of the interview to give a synopsis of what I really wanted to say: That the Gypsies were a people of Indo-European origin, originally from North Central India, who had migrated into Europe by the fifteenth century; and that we spoke a language called *Romanes* or Romani, which was derived from Sanskrit, the ancestor of many of the languages of India, and related to all the Indo-European languages including English.

I also mentioned that Gypsy criminals in Canada should be treated as individual law-breakers and that the group as a whole shouldn't be castigated or held responsible for the actions of an individual. I condemned the racism of the press in that we all too often see headlines such as "Gypsy witch fleeces gullible customer" but never, "English-Canadian sex pervert given five years for child molestation." Why did every other minority have ethnic anonymity in our press except the Gypsy and, I added remembering Marie, the Indian?

She listened to all this and told me that it was good that my people had somebody like me to represent them, to fight their battles for them, somebody intelligent, educated and strong. She felt my muscles as she said this last bit.

"But what do you want the white man to do for the Gypsies?" she concluded.

It had all been for nothing, I thought. Like Marie had said, they'd never take us seriously. They were all too ready to give us their stinking Bibles, toothbrushes and their own brand of lobotomizing education, but they would never give us equality of culture. To this woman, I was nothing more than the native chieftain, Yanko Lee,

King of the Romeo Gypsies as some idiot had already misdefined me in the press. I saw only too well that in the eyes of people like her I was nothing but an interesting human stud, the native who would do all the horrible things to her that a white man wasn't allowed to do. Like Marie was always saying, "They like to screw Indian broads, our red ass is supposed to be horny." I was finally beginning to understand the gentle wisdom of my Black friends and their contempt for "whitey". "The man," they would say, "the man just don't understand."

I concluded the interview as politely as possible and she brought me another beer. I noticed the out-of-scale decorative "schooner" model on her mantlepiece, supposedly the famous *Bluenose*. They sold as Canadiana and were crudely made ornaments manufactured in Nova Scotia. She had the big version that cost over three hundred dollars, but it bore no resemblance to any vessel that had ever sailed the seven seas—illogical rigging, gigantic tiller in place of the proper steering wheel and heavy masts, as thick as fully grown oak trees in proportion to the hull.

I finished my beer and left for Charlie's place. I found a large group of Gypsies assembled there, the women and the girls in their long flowery dresses, the men in new suits. Steve Demitro, the mandolin player, had come along with a group of musicians and about a hundred guests had crowded inside Charlie's small house. Charlie had set a large table covered with hams, chickens, vegetables, fruit, breads of all shapes and sizes along with numerous bottles of beer, hard stuff and wine.

An outsider looking at this abundance of food might think that the Gypsies were rolling in money. They weren't. Most of the food had come from the city mission across the square from Charlie's house and the rest had been conned or stolen from the open air markets along St. Lawrence Boulevard. The Gypsies always got the food for their feasts this way; only the liquor had been bought and it came from Paddy who got it cheap from the hijackers. I saw Paddy and Giovanni sitting with Sergeant Brown who had once been on the local force. Now he was a private detective and acted as a liaison man between the hoods, the whores, the Gypsies and the police. For a price, he could fix up anything short of a charge of first degree murder or bank robbery. He was a jovial man, but inclined to drink rather heavily.

Jilko wasn't at the party; he'd got six months to two years depending on his behaviour. Apparently the plea of temporary insanity had done some good. Kolia hadn't come either. As a European-born Gypsy, he didn't get along too well with the North American-born except for the older ones like Demitro.

The old man was in fine shape and soon got the boys playing and singing; the women danced, and the children laughed, fought and screamed without interference. Mine were somewhere among the bunch and Marie was sitting with the women at the far end of the table, indistinguishable from the rest in her traditional Gypsy costume. The music grew more oriental, the voices more magical and I thought what a strange people we Gypsies were. Here was a scene that could have been taking place almost anywhere in the world, the music, the Romani language, the costumes. As I looked at the towering skyscrapers visible through the open window and tried to visualize the world of the future, perhaps a world without a place for us, an old adage came to mind:

"Where you see Gypsies, there is freedom. Where you do not, there is no freedom."

14

It was early winter, 1965. Kolia wasn't getting much work now and our bills were piling up: light, gas, telephone, but we managed to pay the rent regularly. Marie would be having her baby soon and she needed much better food than we could afford.

Kolia's mother was sick, old age mainly, but Demitro was still in good health. Our dictionary would soon be complete and I hoped that somebody might publish it. This would give us the modest capital needed to start a small machinery repair business.

The more I worked on the dictionary, the more ability I developed. It had already had more local publicity than many published works, but as yet, no serious offers of publication, financial assistance or even serious academic interest. None of my many letters to government agencies or potential private sponsors had produced any results. Czechoslovakia was in the process of compiling a dictionary of the Gypsy dialect spoken there and numerous paid researchers were engaged on it. But nobody, it seemed, was interested in a Canadian dictionary of Romani anymore than a dictionary of one of our many Indian dialects.

I had been working full time as a mechanic for a mail order house which specialized in repairing and selling worn-out and obsolete machinery. It was a sweatshop where immigrants and blackballed Canadians were paid about fifty bucks a week. I was more versatile and was paid sixty dollars to repair machinery, sell on the floor, translate business letters from French or Spanish, run errands and clean out the shithouse periodically. But they'd gone over to selling Japanese imports and slacked off on their sales of domestic junk. The large stock of old machinery was piled up in the basement and insured, for a considerable amount, just before a pipe "burst" and it all became a total loss in the resulting flood. We had worked for three days to carry it all down from the third floor where it had been for the last ten years or more and another three days to carry all the imported junk upstairs. The boss got his money from the insurance company, then bought more new stuff. We'd all been laid off except for one immigrant Greek and some spare-time salesmen. I'd been depending on places like this for my basic income, especially in the winter when I would repair machinery at home, or in the store, for sale in the summer. I'd have to find another source of income now.

This morning I was sitting at home with my left arm in a sling. I'd sprained it carrying the junk downstairs and the doctor had told me to rest for two weeks. So I took the opportunity to catch up on my research and was busy drawing diagrams of ship rigging in one of my many loose-leaf folders. I'd just bought a reprint of a formerly out-of-print textbook, *Seventeenth Century Rigging* by R.C. Anderson. This book, along with the works of Dassié and Aubin, French maritime experts, would complete my research into the rigging of ships in the seventeenth and early eighteenth centuries and enable me to finally construct an accurate model of a ship of this period for my growing collection. Marie peered over my shoulder.

"What the hell is that?" she asked. "It looks like a bunch of spider webs."

"These are the various kinds of crowfoot attachments for the spritsail topmast of a sailing ship in the 17th century," I told her. "Ships of this period had a small mast set up at the end of the bowsprit. This backstay here, with the euphro and the multiple ropes running from it to the forestays is what held it back and prevented the billowing sprit-topsail from pulling it forward and into the ocean. There are special tackles for different periods and different countries. Now I've got the master descriptions, I can go through my drawings and prints and add to them."

"How was the exhibition?" she asked.

"Not much happened," I said. "Last night was closing. Kolia will be bringing my models back from the showroom this morning."

A lot of people had come to look, but nobody made any serious offer. Somebody had wanted to order a dozen of this one or three dozen of that one at fifty bucks a dozen to put in his string of souvenir stands, but once I explained that these are museum standard replicas and I don't do more than one of any given model, he wasn't interested. Even at three bucks an hour, my prices were considered too high. One old lady wanted to buy one for her nephew to sail up in Beaver Lake. People asked me questions like, "Do they work? Will they Float? and Where can I get the stuff to make one like that?" There was one German guy who complemented me on their accuracy, and another Frenchman who went wild over them, but they were just ordinary Joes without money. I thought some of the big shipping magnates or maybe somebody from a museum might approach me but nobody did.

My investment had been for nothing; two hundred bucks gone and nothing to show for it but a lot of happy little boys who saw some ship models.

I would have to sprain my arm now of all times, but thank God it's my arm. That bloody box full of junk could have landed on my fingers instead.

Kolia and Pavlos returned with the collection and brought it into the house. After I'd unscrewed the stands of the models and removed the ships, we put the ships in the old man's room and the empty showcases back into the car for Kolia and Pavlos to return to the rental shop.

Pavlos followed me inside my workshop.

"What are you doing with those paintings, Yanko?" he asked.

"Selling them cheap," I told him. "I'm painting over lithographed representations of sailing ships in oils and doing projections with a magnajector from drawings of ships. It's not art but ship-lovers seem to like them. Anyway, it keeps me supplied in materials and books. They sell fairly well in the art framing shops in the suburban shopping plazas. I'm doing some new ones now, of animals; maybe some rich guy will buy them for his kids' nursery."

Pavlos and Kolia dropped me downtown. I needed some more coloured pencils and a sketch pad. I got the stuff, then went over to the Bistro.

George was there. He told me I was getting bitter.

"Not bitter," I told him, "just plain fed up."

"It's not because you're a Gypsy," he argued. "There's a lot of Wasps in your position, Yanko. There's a hell of a lot of people walking these streets who are nowhere near being what they want to be."

"Are there?" I asked. "Funny, I've been in and out of the Unemployment Insurance Commission for years. I've worked in junk stores and sweatshops; I've done all kinds of low paying menial jobs, but believe you me, buddy, I've never seen a Wasp with my qualifications there."

George didn't seem to understand. For him it was easy with his B.A.

"You seem to take everything personally," he told me.

"Personally!" I said. "Do you think if I didn't have a sick wife and kids to support that I'd stand for this crap. If I was single I'd play havoc with them. I know the ropes now, I've been on the Main for years."

Bill came in and joined us. I told him I was out of work.

"Christ," he sympathized, "with two kids and another on the way and in winter. Some country we live in."

"They don't give a shit about people like me," I told him. "I'm not a Canadian."

"What do you mean, you're not a Canadian," Bill argued. "We played together when we were kids and we got our first piece of nookie the same day from those two sisters up on the Mountain underneath the cross. I didn't even know you were a Gypsy then."

"It didn't mean much, then, Bill," I told him.

"That's the thing about kids," he said. "They all play together but as soon as they get old enough for their first piece of ass they start hating one another. What's the matter with the idiots?"

"Fear of the stranger male," I told him, "Hitler's disease."

At that point Kolia walked into the Bistro, looking for me. He was very worried.

"Yanko," he told me, "my mother is dying."

We left together and drove back to the house. The old man and Marie were sitting at the old woman's bed. The candles in the family shrine were burning and I could smell the *tomuya*, the holy incense of the Gypsies.

"*Merav*," the old lady said, "I'm dying."

She had never complained. If she said she was dying, she was dying. Like all true Gypsies she knew when the *Martya*, or Angel of Death, was standing nearby. She was worried. If she died in the house, the strict Gypsy law would force us to vacate the premises.

"Kolia," she said to her son, "take me to the hospital."

We wrapped her up. She weighed almost nothing. Kolia carried her outside, almost slipping on the powdered snow and ice in the doorway. He put her in the back seat of the car and turned on the heater. We drove to the Hôtel Dieu, the old woman gripping the seat with her gnarled fingers. Willpower alone seemed to be keeping her alive until she could die where she wanted to. The interns rushed her upstairs, but soon a doctor appeared.

"You might as well go to her," he told us.

We went into the room and Kolia knelt down, praying to *Devel*, the Gypsy God. He prayed not to save the old lady, he knew she was finished, but he asked God to accept her into *Raiyo*, the Gypsy Heaven, and to forgive him any evil he might have inadvertently done towards her, that she should bear him no malice in the afterworld. "May I be forgiven of her," he prayed.

I sat down near Doikitsa. She recognized me.

"Yanko," she whispered, as I put my head closer to hers. "Yanko," she said, "take care of Kolia. Now I'm going to God."

She started her death spasms and Kolia grabbed a chair. She clutched one leg while he held onto the other. He was trying to prolong her life for a few more seconds by passing his essence of life through the chair in a last gesture of love. Like the primitive he was, he was trying to contest the unalterable.

The old woman died, falling back onto the bed. Kolia stood silent, still holding the chair.

"Now I leave you to God," he said softly. "*Te soves mishto* – May you sleep well."

The last link with his murdered clan was gone, he was alone. He sat down and cried as I said my own prayer for the old lady.

"What will we do now, Yanko?" Kolia asked, finally. "We have no money for her funeral feasts, for the undertaker, nothing. We can't let the city bury her."

"We'll think of something," I replied. In this crazy country a rich man's dog, cat or canary can be buried in a pet cemetery with a full service, but poor men will be dumped like an alleycat or a dead rat.

We left the hospital to find a priest. Kolia and his mother were not members of any parish, but we finally found a small church where the father promised to do everything for a hundred dollars. We could raise that much somehow. Marie couldn't help us by preparing the funeral feast. She was pregnant and ceremonially unclean; Gypsy law forbade her to touch food intended for guests. Burtya, who was also a distant relative of Kolia's mother, helped out financially and Demitro's family gave the reception after the funeral.

After it was all over, Kolia began to feel morose. He kept telling me that in Europe his people never had much money, but they had always been healthy and happy. Now everything was bad luck. He was sure he had some jinx or curse on him. He pulled out the inside lining of his pocket as we sat at our living room table and a nickel fell on the floor, rolling under the table. My two little girls went after it, and Kolia smiled at them.

He went out alone and Marie joined me.

"Poor Kolia," I told her, "he's alone now. That's something no Gypsy can stand, to be without a family. He can't earn the money he used to and he's starting to drink a lot."

"Money," Marie said. "It's always money. No money, no education; no education, no job; no job, no rent or food. We got the same problem back on the reservation."

"Yes, Marie," I said, in Romani, "*Love kuchiaren e bul* – Money makes the ass shake, especially in Canada."

"But how long can it go on like this?" she said. "How is it the Government doesn't care about anything?"

I thought of Bill, and the words he'd used not long ago.

"What government?" he'd said. "Canada's such a free country we don't even have a fucking Government."

E zelani devlaika, or green goddess, represents the dangerous aspect of the moon, the fatal fascination for the lure of evil. The purpose of the green goddess is to compete with the woman of the right hand path for the soul of man to destroy him through carnalization and cause him to forget his duty towards his fellow man.

This is where Yanko faces this choice and almost succumbs to the lure.

15

The next couple of months things went from bad to worse. Kolia vanished and I could barely make a living. I went from office to office trying to get business machinery to repair or service, but the big companies had most of them under contract. I managed to make enough for food but I was worried about meeting the rent.

It was now the middle of February. I woke up early but stayed in bed, it was warmer there. I could hear the old man puttering around in the kitchen, frying bacon and eggs and making coffee and toast. He didn't feel the cold as much as we did; he'd lived most of his life outdoors.

"Yanko," he called. "Come and eat."

I dressed and we ate after I took Marie her breakfast. She stayed in bed now; her baby was due anytime. The young deaf and dumb girl from up the street had dropped in; she'd found a friend in Marie who was teaching her how to draw. The kid was lonely and somehow Marie could communicate with her.

The doorbell rang. It was István, a Russian Gypsy musician who had recently arrived from Argentina via Mexico. He, his wife, and daughters were famous entertainers, the Demitrievitch family. He'd shown me a scrapbook full of photos and handbills. They'd played in all the big clubs from Paris to London, Buenos Aires and New York, in all the places where Russian emigrés would gather to hear them and remember the past. Their way of life and music had been outlawed by the Communist regime as decadent, and now they roamed the world lamenting their lost homeland. István had been in Montreal for over a month now, but nobody wanted him or his music. A few places were interested, but business was always black in February.

He sat down and had a cup of coffee to get warm, his dark

face was numbed with cold from the sub-zero temperature. He told me that his money had run out and that he'd gone down to the Unemployment Insurance Commission with a temporary work permit to try his luck. He spoke Russian, French, Spanish, German and Romani, and unlike most Gypsies, he could read and write. They'd offered him a labourer's job at forty-five dollars a week loading boxes into trucks in a warehouse. His wife, Lalea, had been offered an engagement in a bump and grind show on St. Lawrence Boulevard but had refused.

He showed me a bundle of files he had with him, wrapped in newspaper. He'd gotten them from a garage to sharpen, but he had no tools and wanted to use mine. After he finished his coffee, I gave him the old metal bath Kolia and I had used for washing pots and pans, and a bottle of muriatic acid. He went out into the backyard, the snow up to his knees; I sat with the old man watching him. He placed the files in the bath, then poured acid over them. In a while, the acid would eat away the accumulated metal filings between the teeth and he could then return them as "sharpened."

"Look at that," I said to the old man, "a man who has played and sung before people like President Roosevelt, General de Gaulle, and the Queen of England, dunking old files into a tank of acid in the backyard of an ex-whorehouse in Montreal to make a few dollars to feed his family for a couple of days."

"Time's running out," the old man said. "It won't be long now."

The doorbell rang again. It was a man from the light company. I owed over thirty dollars on my bill and he'd been sent to collect the money or turn off the service.

"You can't do that," I told him, "the furnace will go off as well. I have a pregnant wife, children and an old man living here."

"O.K.," he said. "I'll tell them you were out. But they'll send somebody else, maybe even later today. They don't let the bills get too high in this neighbourhood."

István got through with the files and brought them back into the kitchen to wash them in the sink. He tried to warm himself over the gas stove. I hated to think of what the gas bill would be, I guessed they'd be around to cut that off too any day now. I'd received my pay-up-or-else letter over three weeks ago.

I left with István. We took the files back to the garage where he collected his pay, six dollars. He offered me a share as was the

Gypsy custom, but I refused.

"*Si ma dosta,*" I told him, "I have enough."

It started snowing again as we walked along Sherbrooke Street towards Guy. István was unshaven, without a winter overcoat, hat or gloves. I was none too respectable-looking either, with shaggy hair, knee boots, heavy ski pants, nylon ski jacket, mittens and a Mountie-type fur cap. I'd thought of a place where István might get some work, a French-Canadian hangout. The owner was an old friend of mine.

We walked along Sherbrooke, past the antique stores. Armour was selling at five hundred dollars a set, old swords for a hundred, flintlock muskets for a hundred and fifty. We turned down Guy, reached the club and ran up the stairs to get warm.

The owner had lived in Paris for many years and knew of István and his family, who were famous there. He didn't hold out much hope for him in Montreal. If he couldn't make it here, I thought, he might as well forget about the rest of Canada.

Sammy, the owner, would let István, his wife and daughters do a sample show that night for twenty-five dollars. If the audience liked it, he would try to give him one show a week until he started to draw crowds, then, a full-time engagement at the regular rates. I knew he was doing István a favour.

We went to István's house where he gave his wife the six dollars to buy food. She rushed out wearing her full Gypsy costume, long dress, silver slippers and a mink coat that had been given to her, István told me, by a wealthy Russian emigrée in Argentina. István picked up his guitar and strummed it softly as we waited. His wife returned, cooked a meal of fried chicken, and made coffee in a large expensive Russian samovar, a family heirloom. He told his wife about the show. Then Katya and Pavlena, his daughters, appeared from another room to eat.

We left early for the club and got some strange looks from the people on the bus. Lalea and the two girls were wearing their traditional Gypsy costumes underneath their fur coats. István had his expensive Russian costume in a valise and I was carrying his guitar.

Once in the club, the owner took us to a table in the back and gave us a free drink while we waited for the show. I could see that business was slack. The show, what there was of it, was terrible. A sexy-looking girl did a poor imitation of Edith Piaf. She was followed by some clod who tried to sing ballads in French-Canadian patois in an even worse imitation of Tex Lecor.

Nobody seemed very much interested as István and his family got onto the stage; he'd changed into his show costume now. They did two numbers, but they were flat. Some drunk started yelling at them, he wanted the stripper coming up next. István turned to look at his wife. She glared at the drunk, put her hands on her hips then raised her right hand in a proud gesture, filled her lungs with air, thrust her shoulders back and burst into a loud song as István accompanied her and the girls joined in. Now they were back on some great concert stage in Europe and I saw them as the old Gypsies had described them in Russia, before the revolution when army officers, students and artists like Tolstoy would come to hear and praise the Zigannas.

The owner thought they were great. He paid István and told him to come back the following Saturday for another show. They left and I remained. I borrowed a few dollars from Sammy and took a table in a dark corner.

"Hello, *gitan*," a woman's voice broke into my thoughts. "Remember me, stuckup?"

She was French-Canadian with obvious Indian blood, about twenty-five, with long black hair and the kind of eyes that look into you instead of at you. She was plumpish, but not too fat and she obviously spent a lot of money at the beauty counter of the drugstore.

"Do I know you from somewhere?" I asked her. Apart from the fact that she was the girl who had sung earlier, I couldn't seem to place her.

She sat down, put her elbows on the table, her chin in her hands and stared into my eyes.

"El Cortijo, Le Vieux Moulin, L'Echourie," she said. "And remember those nice pictures they took when I was sitting on your knee and we weren't wearing any clothes."

It was the kid who used to bug me back in the old days before I met Kolia, the same one that had posed with me for the evidence photos for my divorce.

"But you were a skinny little runt then," I said. "What happened to you?"

She smiled. "I'm a big girl now. I like your Gypsy friends," she went on. "They sing well. But I have a Gypsy soul too, you know, *je suis une vraie gitane.*"

She asked me what I'd been doing and why I had disappeared from my former haunts.

I told her and wished, later, that I'd left out the part about Marie. I finished my beer and decided to leave.

"I'm broke," I told her. "See you around."

She opened her handbag and put a twenty dollar bill on the table beside me. There must have been a couple of hundred in her change purse.

She got up, came around behind me, put her arms around my neck and nibbled at my earlobe.

"*Attend-moi,*" she said softly. "This is my last show."

She left and went onto the stage. Her song was "*Mon Pot le Gitan.*" I looked at her and decided to leave. I had the instinctive fear of the fatal fascination of the left hand path. I looked at the money lying on the table, then put it beside her purse. This girl would be no casual pickup. The owner gave me a funny look as I left.

"Yanko," old Demitro shouted from the darkness of his room as I opened the front door. "Yanko, where have you been?"

I moved to put on the lights. Nothing happened.

"They've turned it off," the old man said.

That meant the furnace had gone off as well.

"Your wife is having her baby," Demitro added casually.

"Where?" I asked him, assuming she'd gone to the hospital.

"In your workshop," came his reply.

Birth, like death, among the Gypsies, cannot take place just anywhere. It must happen outside in a special tent, in a hospital or in some other authorized location. The baby, his mother and the accompanying mess are all agents of pollution to anybody who comes into contact with them.

"Jesus Christ," I said as I rushed into my workshop. Somebody had placed a mattress on the floor and Marie was lying on it with her flannel nightgown pulled up around her stomach. The young deaf and dumb girl stood nearby holding a petrol lamp for light and the baby's head was already protruding from my wife's vagina.

Marie was awake and calm. She smiled at me and told me what had to be done. Like the Indian she was, she knew by instinct and experience. That's the way babies are usually born back on the reservation anyway.

The old man had called the police ambulance, but by the time they managed to fight their way through the blizzard now raging outside I had already delivered the baby, my third child and my first son, to be called István, after his future godfather.

István, my son, born in a workshop surrounded by old typewriters, parts of machines, unfinished ship models and paintings. As we waited, shivering, for the ambulance I looked at my hands now stained with Marie's blood and said a prayer for my son.

"*Te del o Del te na piravel ande muri vulma* – May God grant that he doesn't end up like me."

16

Marie spent a few days in the hospital while I moved out of the house on de Bullion Street. The old man went back to another room in the basement of the brothel next to Charlie's house and I took a small place over on Jeanne Mance, not far from where we'd lived before. Some hippies were just moving out and they left their furniture behind. The new place was big enough for us and I had only the rent to pay, the rest came included. I took this new place under an alias so that the gas and light companies couldn't track me down. We'd lost almost everything on de Bullion Street, but I managed to save the dishes, radio, bedding and other easily moveable stuff including my typewriter, the dictionary, my books, research data and my ship model collection.

The rent of my new place was only fifteen dollars a week; I could make that and food money easily as a full-time fence. What's the use, I figured, there's nothing else now. Even if I did get some low-paying job, the creditors would soon track me down and put a seizure on my salary.

The old man had got nowhere with his Gypsy representation committee; nobody stayed in town long enough to get anything organized. The Gypsies were hopping from city to city, like fleas on a hot stove, trying to find a place of refuge. Those who were smart left the country or became steadily more dishonest. Those who continued to be honest went hungry. The old man was demoralized and was becoming senile. Burtya, the head of the other Gypsy group was a sick man, in and out of the hospital with a bad heart condition.

Marie's anemia was getting worse and I hated to see her pretending that everything was fine, never complaining, overtaxing her strength to run the house and look after the kids.

All the talk now was about the Expo. Spring was on its way and the city was gripped with an insane excitement. It was everywhere, on the radio, T.V., in the papers, it was the main topic of conversation even though this was only 1966. Even the hoods, whores and Gypsies talked of nothing else but the big show, though their interest was much more objective. The whores had it made and the hoods should do well, too. As for the Gypsies, I wasn't so sure. Sergeant Brown, our liaison man, told us that there was talk in official circles of running them all out of town during the season in an effort to clean up the city for the expected army of tourists.

I did pretty good with my hot stuff. People were trying to save money for Expo and there was a ready market for low-priced "second hand" articles. I had an untapped source of customers and made good use of it. Charlie sold mainly to the Gypsies, the whores and hoods around the Main, but having once been respectable, I had a lot of former contacts who were only too happy to do business with me. Even people like Linda and her husband Larry filled their comfortable suburban homes with stuff that I passed on to them. The only reason I didn't make a fortune is that there just wasn't enough quality merchandise coming down the chain to Paddy and Giovanni.

Pavlos, my Greek friend, had finally got his studio. He'd been working for some boys Paddy knew, making sets of pornographic pictures and it hadn't taken him long to get his initial capital.

I went over to his studio to deliver a set of lights he'd ordered and we drank a few beers as we strung them up, listening to the Greek music on the record player I'd sold him.

We finished with the lights and I asked him to drive me over to George's place. I had a portable typewriter for him. I'd have to get a car soon; this fencing necessitated a lot of travelling. George's apartment was on Côte des Neiges; he'd started his promised publicity job with Expo. He invited us in and gave us a beer. His place was well furnished with thick carpets, hi-fi and air conditioning. He examined the machine, but like most writers I've met, he had no interest in quality as far as typewriters are concerned. I'd brought him one of the earliest model electric portables, but he wasn't prepared to expend much on this basic tool of his trade.

"Sixty bucks," I told him, "and that's cheap for a machine like that. It sells for two hundred in the stores."

"But, Yanko," he argued, "an older machine would do just as well."

"George," I said, "I can get a hundred easy for this machine. I already have orders for more than the boys can steal. Look: magic margins, tabulator, power driven typebars, everything. Sixty-five smackers and it's all yours."

"But you told me it was only sixty dollars a few minutes ago."

"It's just gone up," I said. "If you keep me here haggling all night you'll end up paying a hundred. Besides, that machine's got a special history, it could write its own story, maybe a best seller. It was hijacked in the States, then distributed in lots to various wholesalers, then it passed through a few middle men and finally ended up as part of a shipment to Montreal. My two buddies got it from their supplier and now it's here in your little apartment waiting for you to sit down and make yourself a million."

He took it after a brief argument with his pleasant-looking wife. She thought I was a salesman. On their wall I saw the picture of what Expo was supposed to look like. Christ, I thought as I put the money in my wallet, all the money I carry around in this thing and all I get is about ninety dollars a week. But it's more than the junk stores were paying me, at least. If only Paddy could block that leak in the chain we'd all be on easy street.

"How's your boat building?" George asked me, pouring another beer.

"I gave it up," I told him. "I'm doing crap oil paintings now. I just did some on Canada's animals; you know, moose, wolves, beaver, all the animals that we have up in the bush. It's hanging down in the Hunter's Club; they rent it for ten bucks a month, saves storage space that way."

"That's smart," George agreed. "You've got to go with the trends. It's like writing. Once you get to feel the pulse of the literary market in Canada, you've got it made. I'm working on a novel now, about the seduction of a schoolteacher by her pupils. It should go over great."

Poor George, I thought, he didn't only feel the pulse, he had his finger up the arsehole as well.

Pavlos and I left. I invited him to join me for a drink. I'd been avoiding the place where István had played. He'd left town now, for New York where he had friends in the entertainment world.

143

She was there, almost as if she knew I was coming. She wore her club costume, black net stockings, miniskirt, tight white sweater and French beret. She took my hands and looked into my eyes.

"You were a bad boy the other night, Yanko," she told me. "You ran away from me."

Pavlos stared at her as she led me over to a table. Nobody sat there unless she wanted them to. Pavlos obviously wasn't part of her plans by the way she looked at him. He excused himself to go to the washroom.

"Get ride of that creep, Yanko," she said. "He annoys me."

She left to do her show as Pavlos returned.

"Yanko," he said. "Stay away from her."

"Why?" I asked. "All she wants is a good piece of ass."

Pavlos gave me a sad look. "You're starting to talk and act like a hoodlum."

"I *am* a fucking hoodlum," I said, "and so are you."

The girl started singing. Pavlos and I had been driven into the slums to die, but this creature had been born there and had fought her way out.

She left the stage and came back to the table, put her arms around my shoulders from behind and stared past me at Pavlos.

"I'm through for the night," she told me.

"Where are we going?" I asked her.

"Somewhere quiet," came the reply.

"How about the Swiss Hut?" I said with a straight face.

We left Pavlos in the club, then she drove me over to the Hut. There weren't many customers on the ex-beat, now hippie, side where we sat. We drank beer and listened to the jukebox. She had about two and a half quarts to my one. Suddenly Kolia walked in with a French-Canadian painter and his *copine*. I knew them slightly.

"*Oyes amigo*," Kolia called in Spanish. They joined us, Kolia continuing to speak Spanish. He didn't want to identify himself as Gypsy by speaking Romani. He was drunk and I could smell the fumes of the joint he was smoking. His clothes were crumpled and he needed a shave badly.

"Where are you living?" I asked him.

"With Denis here, in a big house in Carré Saint-Louis," he told me. "A lot of us share a house. I have an atelier there. I make

144

handicrafts, vases, flower pots."

Christ, I thought, Kolia a hippie. At least he wasn't a two-bit crook like me. We drank and talked as Cherie, beside me, kept kissing me and rubbing her leg against mine.

"Let's all go for a drive," she suggested.

We got into her car that had been parked in the car lot across the street. Kolia drove; the French-Canadian couple beside him; she wanted the back seat.

We stopped first at a bootlegger on Clark Street just below Sherbrooke where I bought two cases of beer. To hell with those hoods, I thought as I paid him, they can wait for their money.

We left the city on the Laurentian Autoroute. There was a full moon and I thought of how many times Kolia and I had driven along this same highway, to and from jobs in the country.

Sober, Kolia was a good driver, but now he was weaving from one side of the road to the other. He almost sideswiped two cars as he stepped on the accelerator, forcing the needle up to ninety.

Then he turned on the car radio. The strains of "Proud Mary" broke into the nighttime air as we drank, laughed and threw the empty bottles onto the soft shoulder of the highway.

I studied Kolia's face in the rear view mirror. He seemed hypnotized and a tingling sensation ran through the back of my neck.

"Kolia, our souls will wander forever in the darkness of *Kalisferia*," I said in Romani, reminding him of the Gypsy belief about suicide.

He slowed down.

Later, we drove back to the house where Kolia was living. There were beds and mattresses everywhere, a real flophouse. I was soon stretched out on a bed in a small room upstairs. Kolia joined the party downstairs, I could hear them talking as they drank and smoked. Cherie followed me. I could see her silhouette as she undressed in the moonlight. I wanted to sleep but she had other plans. Afterwards, the last thing I remember was Kolia, stoned out of his mind singing the song we'd sung so often in the old days.

"*Molatnivas soro riato,*
Tehara ande diminyatsa,
Makiovavas amalensa
Xasaravas muri viatsa

I was living it up all night,
Until the following morning,
I was getting drunk with my friends
I was wasting my life."

17

I woke up next morning feeling demolished. My mouth felt like the Sahara desert and my head like it belonged to somebody else. I relaxed, in bed, without opening my eyes. Beside me, Cherie's soft, steady breathing told me she was still asleep. My cheek was against her long black hair and one of us stank like hell. The windows were all closed, the atmosphere in the room fetid.

I finally forced my eyes open and stared up at the dirty white ceiling, the cracked plaster and the naked light bulb hanging suspended from a long cord almost directly over my head. It was dark in the room; the curtains were drawn, but I sensed that it must be about noon. I threw the blankets off; I was sweating like hell. My trousers were down around my ankles along with my shorts, my shoes must be on the floor where she'd thrown them last night.

Now I no longer resented Cherie. We were well matched. I thought of her frenzied, off-beat love making, her oral stimulation and savage woman-above position. I wondered how she'd react to more orthodox nookie and got a hard on thinking about it. Well, now was as good a time as any to find out. Nothing like a good piece of ass before breakfast.

I turned towards her but she had her back to me, the blankets drawn up around her. I grabbed her savagely, closed my eyes, turned her around and kissed her.

What the hell is this? I thought as I felt coarse hair against my lips and chin and was suddenly grabbed and thrown back off the mattress out of bed.

"*Sacrement, qu'est-ce que tu fais?*" a heavy masculine voice demanded. "*Je suis pas fifi.*"

It was a young French-Canadian hippie with beautiful shoulder length hair, a bushy beard and a gallic moustache.

"Sorry, buddy," I apologized. "Where's my Gypsy friend?"

"*En bas, dans son atelier,*" he told me.

Kolia was in his workshop, at street level, a large room full of all sorts of junk – paintings, statues, tools, sheets of copper, his *dopo* and Christ knows what else. He was hammering some sort of copper objet d'art into shape over a form stuck into the *dopo*. Two similar items stood nearby, completed. To me they looked like a cross between a spittoon and a flower vase.

"What are those?" I asked him.

"Vases," he told me. "I have an order to make four like this for a hotel, twenty dollars each."

"Did you see my girlfriend leave?" I asked.

"Early this morning," he replied. "There's a note for you in my pocket, here."

I smelt her perfume on the pink paper as I read the note.

"I have to get over to the Swiss Hut right away," I told him. "She wants me there for lunch."

She was sitting with some old clunker, well dressed and obviously wealthy. She introduced me as her brother. He wouldn't know the difference; he was a Polish immigrant who spoke no French and limited English. It was obvious what was going on, her posing as an innocent kid, alone and afraid in the big city, him after what he could get. I could see they'd just eaten a good meal.

The old guy left and she took me to another restaurant for lunch. Later, I asked her to drive me down to Charlie's place. When we got there I told her to wait in her car up the street. Charlie might see her and blab to the old man.

I went into the house and found Paddy, Giovanni, Charlie and Bonnie sitting around the table. Charlie's arm was bandaged and in a sling, Bonnie had a black eye. The house had been smashed to pieces, pictures ripped from the wall and shattered along with the mirrors, the T.V. demolished, the windows broken and almost all the furniture in pieces or otherwise severely damaged. Only the holy icons, the family shrine and the ornate picture on the wall of Jesus Christ had escaped.

"What the hell happened here?" I asked.

"Drinkie drinkie smash smash," Paddy told me.

"Charlie wrecked the joint last night," Bonnie explained. "Got his welfare money, bought some booze and went haywire. Sorry I can't offer you some tea. He wrecked the stove and smashed all the dishes as well."

Charlie sat there looking sheepish. How much can a man take, I thought. I too, could end up like this, I realized.

"I'll have to owe you ten bucks," I told Paddy as I handed him his share of my sales of the day before. "My wife needs some medicine."

He smiled. "God we worry about, Yanko. You we trust."

Charlie finally spoke. "Where the fuck were you, Yanko? The old man's been looking for you. Your wife says you didn't come home last night. What you do, shack up with a whore or something?"

"I had a job with Kolia," I said.

"That crazy D.P. Gypsy back in town?" Charlie asked. "I ain't seen him around for a long time."

Charlie's phone had escaped the holocaust, so I called Marie and told her I'd been working all night with Kolia.

"What took you so long, Yanko?" Cherie asked when I got back to the car.

I shrugged my shoulders. "Business."

She squinted her eyes, looked at Charlie's joint, at Paddy and Giovanni who were just leaving.

"You're a fence, Yanko, aren't you?" she said.

I smiled. "Could be, so what?"

"But that's dangerous, *mon amour*," she said. "I don't want you to take chances."

She opened her handbag and stuffed fifty dollars into my hand. I put it in my pocket. Marie needed to see a doctor.

"*Merci*, Cherie," I thanked her. I was always polite to women.

She turned and stared me straight in the eyes.

"Do you love me, Yanko?" she asked.

"What do you think?"

"But you took so long to come back and see me after you ran out on me, and you fell asleep on me last night," she said. "You made me do all the hard work. Why don't you start being nice to me?"

"Like where?" I asked.

"*Chez moi*," she suggested.

"*Allons-y*," I replied.

She drove up St. Lawrence Main, then along St. Joseph Boulevard going east. It was early spring and she let down the top of her convertible. I sat beside her, admiring her thighs as she drove.

Maybe I'd found my place in Canadian society at last. Her apartment was real fancy, not large, but cozy and well furnished. There must have been five thousand bucks worth of hot stuff, hi-fi, radio, colour T.V., everything. She switched on the hi-fi, Edith Piaf, and I asked for a beer.

"Just one, *mon amour*," she told me. "we can drink later."

She went into her bedroom, came back wearing a silk housecoat over her brassiere, garter belt and black net stockings, changed the record to a dance number and as she threw off the housecoat did one of the numbers she danced in the go-go clubs. I figured this was time for me to earn my fifty bucks so I kissed her. She responded. Then I picked her up and carried her into the bedroom, threw her onto the bed just below the crucifix and, after removing my clothes, went to make love to her.

"No," she said, and rolled away from me. *"Touche-moi pas."*

"You stupid bitch," I yelled at her. "You play up to me, get me all horny for you and now you won't come across."

She gave me a defiant look.

"Cochon," she said.

"You stupid French pig," I told her as I gave her a good whack across the thighs. She yelped in pain or ecstasy and rolled over onto her stomach, hiding her face in the large pillow as I reached for her belt hanging from the wall nearby and proceeded to beat the living shit out of her. What a hell of a way to make fifty bucks, I thought.

"Kurva!" I shouted at her in Romani. "Stupid two-bit whore!"

She rolled over, grabbed me and pulled me down onto the bed beside her; her fingernails sank into my flesh as I threw away the belt. Her face was distorted into a look of savage hunger.

"Viens t'en," she told me. *"Viens t'en,* Yanko, *mon amour, mon gitan."*

I realized now why Linda and I had split up. My first wife had the same complex as this chick. But Ronald Lee, back then, had been far too much of a gentleman to even argue with his wife, let alone knock the daylights out of her with her own belt. Yanko, however, was a savage Gypsy hoodlum who would willingly pound the shit out of the devil himself for fifty bucks.

She writhed and moaned, scratching savagely at my back.

Jesus Christ, I thought, how the hell will I explain the marks to Marie.

"*Envoye*, Yanko," she encouraged me as the facade of the Parisienne melted away to be replaced by the erstwhile Montreal street urchin hidden underneath, "*Envoye*, Yanko, *donne-s'y—pompe mon vieux—plus vite—ah, sacrement.*"

Then we talked and smoked for a while.

"Will you leave me now?" she asked.

"Why should I?" I replied.

"You must think I'm a pig?" she said.

"No," I told her, "*je suis ton pot le gitan.*"

"I've always loved you, Yanko," she went on. "I used to see you in El Cortijo with that funny little guy with the red hair and that big blond English girl. But you never noticed me then. I was always trying to get you to talk to me, to love me."

"You were too young then," I told her, "jailbait."

"But you just raped me a while ago," she said. "I could have you arrested."

I laughed. "With your record, sister, you'd be the last one to go to the cops. Anyway, you're well over the age limit."

She jabbed at me with her lighted cigarette and I caught her hand just in time.

"When did you have your first love affair?" I asked her, "I mean, who busted your cherry?"

"My brother," she told me, "when I was thirteen."

An unlucky number, I thought.

"He was much older than me," she went on. "He taught me to do all kinds of terrible things to him, then he planted me when I was old enough."

Like Alec would say, "Simplicity man, keep it in the family, sort of condenses life."

"Do you hate him?" I asked her.

She didn't answer, I guess she didn't really know. Anyway, the guy must have been a hell of a good teacher.

"Where is he now?" I asked her.

"He's a priest," she told me, mentioning a small parish. Christ, Kolia and I had hit that church once for over three hundred bucks. We used to pass ourselves as platers of holy articles like *solaria* and other religious crap. We'd take the junk into Montreal, have it plated down on Vitré Street, then bring it back and charge the difference. I remembered the young priest too; he'd asked for a cut of our profit.

He knew what the hell we were up to, but, like her, he had a good sense of business.

I saw the time, seven-thirty.

"I'm going home to my wife," I told Cherie. "She'll be worrying about me."

"Meet me after work, tonight, at the club," she asked.

"I'll try," I told her. "But I can't promise. I got lots of things to do."

"Do you have enough money?" she asked me as I got up and started to dress. "I don't want you to take any more risks selling stolen goods."

"You just gave me fifty bucks," I said, "remember?"

She followed me into the living room, naked, picked up her handbag from the coffee table, opened it and stuffed about thirty-five dollars more into my jacket pocket. Then she handed me a set of keys.

Christ, I thought, I was finally in the right profession. I'd already got a raise and the keys to the executive washroom.

"Thanks a lot," I told her.

Marie was in our living room knitting something for one of the kids.

"How was the job?" she asked me after we kissed.

"Made about eighty bucks," I told her as Delilah, my oldest daughter, grabbed at my leg wanting to be picked up and István, my son, stood up in his crib holding the bars.

"It's a really big job this time," I went on. "I'll have to go back quite a few times to finish it. It'll all be nightwork, though," I warned her. "It's too hard to get access to the machinery in the daytime."

I gave my wife the money. "Now you can go to the doctor," I told her. "I'll have more by the weekend."

She looked at me with that look of love that I know so well.

"I always knew you and Kolia could work well together," she said proudly, "and he always seems to show up when you need him."

"Yes," I said, "we must share the same destiny."

— 18 —

The next few months passed quietly. I kept on working with Paddy and now I had a nice new convertible, hers, to deliver the stuff. Cherie let me use it while she was working; I'd pick her up afterwards.

The dictionary was now completed. I found the time somehow, and I took it down to the old man in the basement room of the cathouse. The women had started to move out now, heading for the downtown area where they could rent cozy, centrally located apartments after the landlords had thrown out the pensioners, students and factory workers; the whores paid more.

Paddy and Giovanni were worried, the big boys were moving in from the States. Already about forty kingpins in the local underworld had been found shot to death. The American torpedoes were efficient.

"It'll seep down even to little guys like us," Paddy told me. "When the Cosa Nostra move in, they overhaul the whole organization." The delegated *capo* had already arrived and set up his office downtown with his legal department and liaison experts. Expo was big money, big enough to attract direct manipulation. Normally the crime syndicate just took their cut from the local boys, but now they wanted to supervise the whole operation to avoid wastage, inefficient handling of potential source of revenue, and possible feuds among the local boys that could result in bad publicity and loss of income.

The old man went through the dictionary, then packed his personal copy in his travelling trunk which had now been moved into his basement room.

"We'll go to Ottawa soon," he said proudly, "and get it copyrighted."

We went next door to Charlie's house. Paddy was there with Charlie. He told me that Giovanni had left town in a hurry, then asked me to be his partner.

"It's easy," he told me. "But I need a cool, reliable man I can trust. I got a B and E job lined up for this afternoon, but I can't do it alone. I need somebody to drive the car."

"No thanks," I told him.

Peddling stuff was one thing but burglary was another. I preferred to keep the rope below the waist. Fines were one thing, jail was another. Anyway, Gypsies are chiselers, not thieves.

"Be careful, Yanko," the old man told me in Romani. "It would be bad publicity for our dictionary if one of the authors was arrested."

"Help me with this one job," Paddy begged. "My rent's overdue, my wife's sick again and I need money badly."

I did owe Paddy many favours. He'd loaned me money in the past, especially when I had to leave the house on de Bullion Street and take another place in a hurry.

"O.K.," I agreed, reluctantly. "I'll help you with this one job, but that's all. Find somebody else for your next one."

Paddy thought he had it all figured out. I dropped him and saw him enter the house in the Town of Mount Royal. But something went wrong. When I came back to pick him up I saw the stakeout. He tried to run for it, but the detectives dropped him after firing a warning shot in the air. He'd been carrying his briefcase under one arm and a parcel under the other, a mink coat wrapped inside. He couldn't have shot even if he'd had a gun on him.

I drove off in a hurry and ditched the car as soon as I could. I opened the glove compartment to see if there was any evidence that might connect Paddy with Charlie or me. There wasn't much inside, a map, a ballpoint, an envelope containing snapshots of his wife and kids and his gun, a colt 45. I stuffed it in my belt, under my sportscoat. Whatever happened to me, Marie and the kids would be looked after by the Government. As for me, I had no intention of going to jail.

I went to the Hunter's Club where my animal paintings were on display. That's the last place the cops would look if they were after me. It would also give me the chance to make a few phone calls to see if anybody had been asking questions. I could stay with Cherie if I had to - nobody knew about her - and stay out of sight until I found out where I stood. I'd been wearing sunglasses and even if they'd seen me, I could always get a brushcut, change my clothes, even find a dozen Gypsy witnesses to testify that I'd been in Toronto for the last week. I was safe unless Paddy talked, but I knew he wouldn't. Perhaps he was even glad it was now all over. He wasn't a violent desperado, just a man with next to no education and no trade, an ex-carnival operator with a large family to feed. Now they'd get public welfare. He'd kept the gun only to shoot the tires of any police car that might have been chasing him. He would never have shot a cop, not Paddy.

The Hunter's Club wasn't too crowded and nobody seemed to pay much attention to me. The manager gave me a free drink and the ten dollars rental for the month. Then, a bit later, he introduced me to a well-dressed guy with thick, horn-rimmed bi-focals.

"Are you Mr. Lee?" he asked.

I took a while to hear him. I'd used so many aliases in the last few years and my close friends called me Yanko. Ronald Lee, the would-be ship model builder and maritime historian was a long time ago in a world of hope and enthusiasm, hardly to be connected with this pimp sitting here with a loaded 45 stuffed into his pants under his jacket.

"Yes, I am," I told him.

He sat down.

"I like your paintings," he informed me. "Good stuff. That's the sort of thing we're looking for."

This couldn't be the cops, I thought.

He went on to ask me about my background, education, places I'd worked, my family and what not, and I wondered where all this talk was leading. I gave him a respectable account of what I was and he seemed satisfied.

"Will you be home about noon tomorrow?" he concluded.

"Yes," I replied. I was planning to stay put for a while.

"Good," he said, "we'll be contacting you soon."

We shook hands and he left. Then I went to the phone and called Charlie. It was bad news. The grapevine had it that Paddy had been shot in the liver and was in hospital under guard. The police had been tailing him but they were looking for Giovanni, not me. I realized that with my sunglasses, hat and dark complexion I could easily have been mistaken for the Italian. We were about the same size.

I had a few more beers, relaxing now that I knew I was in the clear, and stared at my animal paintings lining the walls. Christ, I never thought anybody would take them seriously as genuine art. Later, I went over to see Kolia. His atelier was in a hell of a mess and he was drunk. I told him what had happened as he gave me a quart bottle of beer from the case lying on the floor.

"*Carrajo*," he said, "you were lucky. I told you not to get involved with those *Gazhe* crooks. What will you do now?"

"I guess I'll have to become a real hood," I told him. "Now Paddy's gone there's not much else for me. I know some smart boys on the Main, not small-time guys but real gangsters. They like me and they've already asked me if I want to go into the rackets. Why take chances with hot stuff for peanuts when you can go big time; with my languages and abilities I could go high. We're too honest, Kolia. That's our trouble. We're nibblers. If you want to get ahead in Canada you've got to think big. Gun some fucker down, grab his loot and set yourself up in his place. I've been stupid, I've wasted half my life looking for recognition, human decency, success through hard work. Bullshit, now I'm going to make up for lost time."

"That's blood money, Yanko," he said. "We Gypsies don't do those things."

"No, we don't," I told him. "We're nothing but a bunch of penny ante chiselers and con men. Why don't we fight for a country of our own like the Israelis instead of running all over the world to get away from people who are out to destroy us and our way of life. We think we're smart when we clip some *Gazho*, smart like hell. Why don't we take guns, bombs and fight for our own fucking country. Long live Romanestan! Freedom or death! To hell with the *Gazhe*."

He wouldn't concede the point. If God didn't choose to grant him good luck, then he would accept the bad. Like all his people, he was deeply religious within the framework of his own Gypsy beliefs.

As we talked, he grew drunker and kept reminiscing about the good times we used to have in the past, the jobs, the wild parties and the jokes, like the time we conned the guy out of all that food. I felt sad as I saw him sitting there trying to drown his memories in alcohol. I had to leave.

I got up and adjusted my trousers. The weight of the revolver was pulling them down on the left side. I took the gun and removed one of the slugs from the cylinder. Now if it went off accidentally the hammer would fall on an unloaded chamber, thus preserving my manhood.

Kolia saw the gun; he said nothing.

"*Ash Devlesa,*" I told him, "Stay with God."

"*Zha Devlesa,*" he replied, "Go with God."

I went over to Cherie's place. She wouldn't be home yet, but I had the keys. I walked up to the door of her apartment building. This time the key didn't fit the lock. I'd used it before, it must fit. I tried again, no luck. Then I examined the key and saw that it wasn't hers. A long time ago Marie had given me a large brass key. As I stared at it, I realized this was Marie's way of telling me that she knew the truth.

Shaken, I sat on the steps of the apartment building. I had failed her. She was dying slowly and my kids were living in poverty. I looked at the sky overhead. The searchlight on top of Place Ville Marie, as it made its sweep across the city, looked almost as if it was the prototype of some new and deadly ray that would one day be installed to seek out and destroy the last remaining pockets of freedom and humanity in my city. I said a soft curse in Romani.

"*Te meren ando tumaro kul* – May you all die in the filth of your own making."

I wanted to fight back, somehow, to form an army of all those who had wanted to be Canadians, to help build a great country, but had been shut out, had been branded "Negroes," "Indians," "Gypsies," "radicals," "crackpots" and "commies" in a Canada where the only true Canadian must be white, English Christian and believe in Easter Bunnies, tooth fairies, football and one white man being worth twenty of any other kind.

I found myself heading for the Bistro. They were all there. I stood beside the table looking at them: Bill, the radical agitator; George, the journalist; Etien, the separatist; Joe, the drifter; and the rest.

"Your rotten cocksuckers," I said, swaying drunkenly. "You all know what's wrong with this fucking country and do nothing. Wake up, you sons of bitches, and do something before it's too late."

Bill looked at me as if he'd seen his dreams come true. He jumped up and embraced me like a brother.

"Men," he roared in his Dominion Square-style rhetoric. "Men, the revolution is at hand, the voices are rising in protest. Down with the system. That's what I've been telling you cunts for years. Smash the exploiting swine! Long live the Canadian revolution!"

"Long live the Canadian revolution!" I agreed, pulling Paddy's revolver from my belt and flourishing it in the air.

"Christ almighty," Bill said. He grabbed my arm, pushed me into the one empty booth in the place, wrested the gun away from me and stuffed it inside his pants under his jacket.

"Put that fucking this away, Yanko," he told me. "It's not time for guns yet."

Everybody at the table laughed.

"Never mind those cattle," Bill said, putting his arm around my shoulders. "Our day will come, comrade." Then he added as the waiter passed, "garçon, two beers."

O bango wast, the left hand path, also the devil, represents the man who has chosen to employ his share of the universal intellect and his power for purposes of evil. This man worships evil through its archangel, monetary power, and uses this power to cause human suffering, to destroy human potential and create general misery. There cannot be rich and powerful men if there are no poor. Here we see the burning firebrand and the snake wrapped around the knife. The demon sits aloof on his mountain gloating over his rising pile of shekels, contemptuous of the human condition of his fellows so long as his wealth and power remain inviolate.

This is where Yanko learns the answer to the riddle of life and confronts the actual devil and arch enemy of mankind.

— 19 —

I woke up next morning with a real hangover. Bill and I had got stinking drunk and sung all the revolutionary songs we could think of, making up words as we went along. It was hot in my small apartment with its little rooms. We were on the third floor and had a back gallery, which we shared with the other tenants of the building. It wasn't much use to us. The guy next door was always coming home drunk at all hours of the day and leaving the gate open, so that my kids, and his, could fall down the three flights of stairs to the stone yard below. Just a few days ago, my baby son, István, had been lying out there on his blanket and he'd almost rolled to the end of the gallery. Marie had spotted him just in time. Our place felt like a sardine can and I hoped we'd be able to move into a larger flat or house before we all went mad. But with kids it was now becoming almost impossible to rent a decent flat or house at a normal rent.

Marie had got up before me, she was sitting in front of the window. I was still wearing my shirt, pants and socks. She must have removed my jacket and shoes last night after Bill brought me home in a taxi. I went over to her.

"Hi," I said, putting my arms around her.

"Want some tea?" she asked.

I could tell by her vibrations that she was thinking about Cherie.

She went into the kitchen. I could hear my kids fighting in their little prison. Then she brought my tea.

"You know," I said.

"For a long time," she answered.

"And?" I asked.

"That's up to you, Yanko," she said. "Which one of us do you want? You can't have both."

"There was never anybody but you," I told her.

"You gonna see her again?" she asked.

"No," I said. "I'm free of her now. She's just part of this rotten world we're living in, I guess I was just trying to destroy myself."

I told her about Paddy.

"He was a good man," she said, sadly. "That bitch know you were married with kids?" Marie had a one-track mind.

"She never asked me anything about you."

Marie shook her head sadly. "It wouldn't have been so bad if she'd been an Indian, or a Gypsy woman."

I put my arms around her. "My little squirrel. You know I love you."

"And I *understand* you," she said.

"We're going away," I told her. "To Mexico. I'll get Kolia, he's still got an old jalopy. We're going back on the road. We'll work our way through the States. There's lots of Gypsies in Mexico living the old life, Kalderash, like Kolia and me."

"What about the old man?" she asked.

"He's too old," I said. "Anyway, he'll never leave the whorehouse as long as Charlie is next door. Nine sons and not one of the bastards can give the old fellow a decent place to live. Will you mind leaving Canada?" I concluded. "You're an Indian, this is your country."

"I have no country," she said. "It was stolen a long time ago."

Through the window I noticed a car drive up and stop in front of our apartment building. What the hell was a Bentley doing in this neighbourhood? I glanced at my watch. It was noon. A uniformed chauffeur got out and came up the steps of my building. The buzzer of my apartment sounded. I went into the hallway and pushed the button to open the door. He came up, panting and wiping the perspiration from his forehead with a handkerchief.

"Does Mr. Ronald Lee live here?" he asked me.

"That's me." I told him.

"My employer wants to see you," he informed me. "Can you come now?"

This wouldn't be the cops, I thought. Then I remembered the man I'd met in the Hunters' Club the night before.

"Can you wait till I change?" I asked him.

Whoever the hell his employer was, I didn't want to meet him in the clothes I'd just slept in.

I picked out a tropical suit I'd bought from Paddy, along with a clean shirt, tie, socks and my best pair of shoes.

"I'll phone you later," I told Marie as she stood, puzzled in the doorway watching as we left.

The neighbours stared from their galleries, probably wondering what the hell that Gypsy bum with the squaw was doing in an expensive English car. The chauffeur drove to an impressive looking house in Upper Priests' Farm.

I followed him inside, to a large expensively furnished study where his employer was waiting. He was dressed in a pair of baggy flannel trousers, running shoes in the last stage of their existence and an old shirt. He sported a handlebar moustache and needed a haircut.

"Sit down, Mr. Lee," he invited. "You may leave now, Harold," he said to his chauffeur.

He offered me a cigarette and lit it with an ordinary wooden match from a large box on the desk beside him. A hood or a sweatshop owner would have flashed an expensive lighter. He didn't introduce himself, he didn't have to. He told me that he was an avid hunter, associated with numerous hunting clubs all across Canada. I saw the trophies and hunting rifles on the walls of the den: lion heads, tiger heads, tusks. Christ, I thought, the guy even goes on safari. There were Queen Anne glass cases around the room full of expensive hand-made figurines of wild animals. On his desk he had one of a caribou, which he kept toying with as he spoke to me.

Apparently his "group of friends," as he called them, had decided to do something for Expo 67. They wanted to set up a privately sponsored, unofficial exhibit dedicated to the preservation of our Canadian wildlife, aimed both at interesting the common Joe in hunting and in preserving our animals.

"We must preserve, at all costs, this great national heritage of ours," he explained, fidgeting with his caribou.

"Many species of animals are being forced into extinction today and we must do everything possible to save them. Others are being decimated and driven out of their natural habitat by predators. Animals that have developed certain habits and instincts cannot survive if they are suddenly and ruthlessly transplanted into a foreign environment or if they are struck by disease from man's pollution."

Listening, I felt suddenly indignant as I thought of my wife and family, the Gypsies, Indians, and all the poor in the slums.

"I knew you were an animal lover, Mr. Lee," he told me. "Your paintings tell the story. Only a man who truly loves animals could portray them with such artistry. You're a real Canadian to love our animals as you do."

He handed me the figurine of the caribou.

"Some Italian chap picked it up in Italy," he said. "Isn't it beautiful? Our largest animal and king of the Canadian north. We're having a contest soon to shoot the largest we can for our main exhibit. It will be stuffed and shipped to Montreal in ample time for the opening. All the big hunting clubs and the Government are co-operating. I have created a little team, so far, all employees of mine from my various plants, but I need someone like you, someone who knows and understands animals."

Christ, I thought. What was this guy leading to?

"Would you be interested in the position of theme director?" he asked. "I plan to continue the exhibition and take it on tour across Canada, to the United States and over to Europe to encourage immigration. It could be a permanent job. Our funds are somewhat limited, but I can offer you two hundred dollars a week to start."

I was stunned. The position had all sorts of possibilities. I might get to meet important people in the museum field, people who would understand and appreciate my model building. Maybe this man himself would help me once I showed him my work and explained what I was trying to do. Now, after all the years of struggling, maybe things would change. I saw a way out of my prison.

I accepted his generous offer and my new employer took a group of figurines from the showcases, put them on his desk, and explained more or less what his exhibition was all about.

It would consist of stuffed animals in their natural surroundings, in large, plexiglass cases—"kinderproof", as he called them. There would also be my paintings plus others, photographs of typical hunting scenes and life-sized dioramas, store dummies dressed as hunters, trappers or anglers set in typical single or group scenes.

"I hear from Kenneth at the Club that you haven't been working too regularly," he told me, "just making ends meet."

He handed me an envelope.

"We all go through these periods," he said. "This will tide you over until your first pay cheque comes through. I'll have somebody pick you up tomorrow and you'll be more or less your own boss over there, except that Tom Smith, who is in charge, is responsible for the whole operation. Smith will tell you what to say if anybody asks you who you're working for and who's paying your salary. Never mention me. I'll deny I ever heard of you. There are reasons for this, but we don't need to go into that. Just do what Smith tells you to and there won't be any problems."

He rang the bell for his chauffeur.

"Harold, take Mr. Lee back to wherever he wants to go," he told him. "He's joining us."

"Oh, by the way," he said to me, as I got up to leave, "I read your article in the Canadian Free Press. I don't think you'll be needing your Romani in this job. English and French will be sufficient."

I asked "Harold" to drop me at the Bistro, where I joined Bill who'd dropped in for late lunch.

"Get over last night O.K., Comrade?" he asked. "Boy, you really got loaded. But I'm glad you've finally joined us."

He handed me a heavy brown parcel from his briefcase. He'd taken a risk carrying it around for me.

"Put that fucking thing away, Yanko, and keep it out of sight," he told me. "Guns are easy to get. We need more people first."

I ordered a beer, then remembered the envelope the man had given me. I opened it, Christ almighty, five hundred dollars. Bill watched me as I counted it, his eyes wide with amazement.

"What the hell have you done, Yanko?" he asked, glancing nervously around him.

I told him of my good fortune.

"Now I'll be recognized," I concluded.

"Recognized," he exploded, "Christ, you're an expert on historical ships, not a taxidermist. Who the hell recognized you? The public, a panel of experts, the Canada Council? Who is this rich guy anyway, he sounds like the Establishment?"

"He probably is," I said. "But what the hell's the Establishment? I see it as a chance to be accepted eventually for what I really am."

"By him?" Bill said, "and others like him? Don't sell yourself short, Yanko, don't let them buy you. They always find ways to undermine serious radical types. Get wise to them."

"But they're not buying me," I argued. "They're paying me to do a job. They just pay a bit more than most people."

"And where do they get their money?" he said. "From the struggling masses. They're capitalist swine."

"Oh, fuck your politics," I said. "All I want to do is make ship models and study history. I don't give a shit for all this rubbish. I want to do something useful in life."

"Like stuffing a bunch of animals?" he asked.

"I can show him my models," I argued.

"Show him your models?" Bill said. "Why don't you show him the alchies lying in the parks; maybe his product put them there. Or the whores around the Main; maybe his puritanical theocracy drove them there. Or the unemployed; maybe his automation took their job. But he doesn't want to see that. He wants to save his pretty animals because his own rotten system is falling. He thinks that if he can save the vanishing animals he can save his vanishing system. But it won't work, Yanko. The revolution will succeed in the end and their rotten system will collapse."

"Oh, what the hell," I said. "Count me out of this. All I want to do is get somewhere with my model building."

Bill's voice became louder. "Another good man bought out. Christ, Yanko, you had all the makings of an ardent revolutionary last night and now you've sold yourself."

George came in and joined us. He showed us a story with photographs he was working on, about a belly dancer. He was confident that he'd sell it for a good price.

"That's it," Bill said. "You go stuff your animals and he'll write about belly dancers and cock teasers. It's hopeless, the revolution is doomed."

"I'll drop over to see you," George told me after I'd given him the lowdown on my new job. "I'll do a story on you and this animal thing."

I went home and told Marie.

"What about Mexico?" she asked.

"I'll work at this new job for a while," I told her, "and see what happens. We can save a lot of money and if things don't work out we can always go somewhere else."

"What about Kolia?" she asked.

"He can take care of himself," I told her. "He always has."

"What can I say," she told me. "I want you to be happy, to succeed, Jesus Christ, you deserve it. But those animals, *gadzum*. But if you think this will get your models known and help you out to do what you've always wanted to do, I'm all for it. I'm just afraid it might destroy you," she said.

"Destroy me, at two hundred dollars a week?" I said.

"Yanko," she began, "you're not like most men. The average guy would take his money and do whatever he was told to do. But you won't. You'll end up getting disgusted when you see the way those rich people act."

"What do you know about rich people?" I asked.

"My two sisters were maids," she said. "Lots of Indian girls work as maids. Where do you think the blue-eyed Indians come from? The orphanages are full of them."

"I have to tell the old man," I said. "At least he'll be happy for me."

I called him and waited while Charlie sent one of his kids into the whorehouse to get him.

"This is good," he said. "Now you won't have to take chances any more. You'll be working for those important gentlemen. You can talk to them about the dictionary, about the Gypsies and what should be done to stop them from destroying themselves in the slums."

Charlie wasn't happy the same way, I learned later. The moment he learned of my success, I crossed the line. I became the enemy, the system. Soon I would no longer be welcome on St. Lawrence Main. My home could be burglarized and Charlie would gladly sell the stuff for Vladimir and Pierre, the two guys who had taken over Paddy's old circuit.

— 20 —

Next morning I started my new job. Tom Smith picked me up and drove me over to the exhibit. I was the theme director, but Smith was the man over everybody. He was about forty and he'd been a foreman before the boss sent him to the exhibit. He had to have a title so he was called "curator", whatever the hell that meant.

"What about them paintings?" Smith asked me as we strolled around the exhibit building. "The boss wants 'em picked up soon as possible before sumthin' happens to 'em."

I told him where they were, then called the Hunters' Club to tell them that somebody would be down to pick them up.

Smith dispatched one of the contractors with a panel truck. He came back an hour later with the paintings loaded into his van along with a load of toilet fixtures.

"Picked up some shithouse equipment for Expo," he told Smith. "Ain't no use making two trips, is there?"

"When all the junk has got here," Smith explained later, "we'll go through it, throw out what's no good and put the rest on show. That's your job, buddy."

"How will we know what to exhibit?" I asked.

He smiled. "Easy, nuthin' to it. Whatever the boss wants. He'll come down and go through the junk. What the boss wants, we keep; what he don't want, we get rid of."

"What am I supposed to do?" I asked him.

"Nuthin', Lee," he replied. "We ain't ready for you yet. The boss'll let you know when he's ready. Go take a look at Expo, see what's going on there."

Our exhibition was outside the Expo site proper and I saw an army of guards checking on people going in.

"Do I need a pass or something?" I asked.

"Oh, yeah. You gotta get your mug shot. You can go to the photographers with Harry there, the carpenter. He'll drive you."

The carpenter took me downtown and stopped in front of a photographic studio.

"Tell Smith we got stuck in the traffic, O.K.?" he said as I got out. "I wanna whip into the tavern."

After I left the studio I went for a haircut. Maybe I should have got one before the picture, but I wanted a souvenir of the way I looked before my symbolic emasculation. Long hair, beards and sideburns are the mark of wisdom, masculinity and revolution. Canadian man, like Samson, has to be ceremonially castrated if he is to serve the Establishment rather than challenge it.

What a joke, I thought, two hundred bucks a week and so far, nothing to do. I went over to the Bistro and met George.

"Hey, Yanko," he said, "I just came from your animal exhibit. Some clod in a leather jacket and jeans told me you'd just left."

"That's my boss, Tom Smith," I told him.

George handed me some papers.

"I got the background for my article on you," he said, "but I need some more facts."

"I wouldn't say I was a Gypsy," I told him.

"Why not? I think it adds colour."

"It will stereotype me," I told him. "An English-Canadian can be a painter, poet, writer or sculptor, but not so a member of a minority group. With us, the ethnic label always comes first, Negro-lawyer, Indian-wrestler or French-Canadian-author. I don't want to end up being called a Gypsy-animal-stuffer. Just say I'm a Canadian, O.K., poor kid from the slums, worked since age 15, went to night school, all that, you know me."

"O.K., but I really don't think it would do any harm. After all, people don't usually associate Gypsies with theme directors of Expo."

"If you want to crucify me, use a hammer and nails, not your typewriter."

"Don't get excited, Yanko," he said. "I know Gypsies. I've read through your manuscript on the Gypsy culture, but readers like angles, gimmicks, colour, not hard facts."

I told him a few other things to leave out like my Indian wife and my long association with hippies and other colourful St. Lawrence Boulevard types.

176

"For Christ's sake, Yanko," he argued. "You're castrating my article."

"Whatever happened to your serious stuff, George?" I asked.

He gave me a look, sort of whimsical.

George, too, had his story. Unlike me, he came from a well-off family. He'd have had it made if he'd gone into the family business. But he wanted to write. In the past, he'd written dozens of satiric articles, even completed a novel on the absurdity of the Canadian myth. But it hadn't sold and gradually, he'd found his way through trial and error, rejections and suggestions for rewrites to the type of thing that does sell. Now he was successful, but somewhere along the line the old George I'd known sitting up all night typing away in his basement room on St. Famille had died.

I left George and went over to see Pavlos, my Greek photographer friend. I found him in his studio working on his new photography magazine.

"The first issue is ready to go to the printers," he told me. "I've got photos from all over Canada by different people. Some are very good."

"What else are you working on?" I asked.

"Those." He pointed to a pile of nudes on the table, not pornography this time, but artistic nudes. Christ, I thought, he must have emptied the Bistro of would-be fashion models to get these. I recognized a lot of the girls by their faces, but I'd never realized how skinny they were with their clothes off. I'd have to put him in touch with some hefty whores I knew.

"What do you figure to do with these?" I asked him.

"Put them on exhibition," he told me. "Then I'm going to Greece for a while, to take a whole series, sort of put Kazantzakis and the other Greek writers against a background of Crete, the villages, the people. A man who might be connected with the art exhibit in the Greek pavilion at Expo told me somebody there might be interested."

"You'd better get something a bit more substantial than that," I told him. "What are you doing about rent?"

He frowned. "I've got good credit."

I glanced through his pilot magazine, a series of pictures including some that he'd taken of Gypsies in Montreal, their homes in the slums, the old man, the fortunetellers and the kids playing among the garbage cans. It even had something I'd written a long time ago.

"Who the hell is going to go wild over stuff like this?" I said. "It isn't Canadian."

"But it's life," he argued. "Life right here in Montreal, the life you've been living. I was at that party you describe in the poem, where Burtya, the patriarch, got drunk and fell on the floor and his wife fainted from the heat. Those Gypsy kids eating oranges, the old man crying, I've seen it all."

"I know," I said tiredly, "but what does this mean to some guy in Toronto, or Vancouver, or Halifax? This stuff is too alien for the common Joe. It won't sell."

"It can't be that bad," Pavlos argued.

"Canadians are a race of do-it-yourselfers. They see the Mona Lisa and they buy a set of painting by numbers to make their own copy. They see a complete scale fully rigged rib-and-plank model of a hundred-gun ship of the line of 1675 and they rush out to buy a carving knife and a lump of balsa and maybe some Canadian flags to stick on their masterpiece. Every myopic clod has his own Japanese camera and every young bitch with a big pair of knockers and a sexy ass is a movie star. That's why this country's in a mess. Anybody can be the Prime Minister and any ex-general with one leg, one eye or one nut can become Governor General. Who needs an impressive record of public service? Christ, Pavlos, if you apply for a job sweeping floors they ask you for a degree in sanitation engineering and at least ten years Canadian experience, but if you want the job of running Canada all you need to be is a teetotaller."

"But Expo will make people more cultured and more aware of the arts."

"Arts!" I said. "Pavlos, there's a vicious gang war going on right now between two local syndicates. One group is topless and the other is bottomless.

Typical scene, washroom of a Montreal tavern, two guys standing at the urinal taking a leak:

'Hey, Buddy, you a tit guy or an ass guy?'

'Ass guy, what's it to you Mack?'

BANG!

'Sorry, Buddy, I'm a tit guy. No hard feelings.' "

I left the studio and went to where I figured Cherie would be at this time of day. I had some unfinished business to attend to.

"Where have you been, Yanko?" she asked. "I thought you might be sick, or something. But I couldn't come to your house, your *sauvagesse* wouldn't like that, would she?"

"No. She certainly wouldn't."

I laid the keys on the table in front of her. Not that I figured she needed them. It was a symbolic gesture of finality.

"So you don't want me anymore?" she said.

I smiled. "I just got a better job."

She stared at me. There are no words to describe the look. She was the one who usually terminated the contract and took back the keys. Her face contorted into a look of frustrated anger as she whispered the words through her clenched teeth:

"*Maudit gitan*," she said, then repeated it in English for emphasis, "You goddam Gypsy."

21

Progress at Expo slowed down during the winter, then picked up again in the spring of '67. We rushed like maniacs to get everything ready. Stuff began arriving by the truckload; stuffed animals, dummy duck decoys, equipment, canoes, tents and God knows what else.

I hadn't seen the boss since he'd hired me, but another guy had appeared to direct our efforts. Percy Steadman usually showed up half-plastered, but he told us everything had to be ready by April 1st when the boss and the other backers were coming to see the results of their expenditures.

Marie and I had rented a large old flat on Park Avenue with seven rooms and a large picture window in my study which faced onto the street. It was a real palace after the dumps we lived in for so long. We had now become respectable and even my half-brother whom I hadn't seen for years dropped in occasionally. He was five years younger than me and still single. He had a good job as a bookkeeper and now that I was back in the fold he'd decided to resume the family ties.

I did eventually get three ship models exhibited at Expo; they were to appear outside the movie theatre in the Canadian Pavilion along with a motley assortment of Canadian artifacts like Indian tomahawks, spinning wheels, cart wheels and horse shoes, and not in the artistic section with the finger paintings, lumps of jagged metal, and polished rocks.

My new home had become a centre for my new friends, many of whom were connected with Expo in one way or another. The Gypsy boys used my home for parties; almost every weekend a gang would show up with electric amplifiers, guitars, mandolins and bongo drums. When there was no party, my friends and the Gypsies would drop in one after the other, often overlapping, and spend an hour or three chatting. The trouble was that there were so damned many of them that there always seemed to be somebody there. If they couldn't make it in the flesh, they'd phone. Marie and I had to go out to be alone.

She was much healthier now, but she was disgusted with the whole thing. We'd finally got a nice place, well furnished and all, and I had a beautiful workshop, well set up with power tools and equipment, but I was doing nothing with it.

The best of my new friends was Draža Sudić, a giant Canadian of Serbian ancestry with a fierce moustache. In an age of revolution he was a fervent monarchist and wanted to see the king restored to Yugoslavia. He spoke many languages and was a liaison man with a bureau connected with international tourism and accommodation of Expo visitors. His passion was Balkan music and to his way of thinking, the Serbs, the Greeks and the Gypsies were God's chosen peoples.

Sudić hated England with a deadly enmity. He fully believed that Churchill had sold out Mikhailovitch and the Royalists to Tito and the Communists, whom he hated more than he hated Churchill. Turks came next on his list of enemies and he would talk longingly and nostalgically of the great battles between the Turks and the Serbs in times past. He'd grown up in Canada listening to his father playing the old epic ballads on the *gusla*, telling of these exploits.

During working hours he paid lip service to the Canadian myth and in the evenings and on the weekends danced his savage Serbian dances or sang his battle songs to the music of the *gusla*. We would often go to the Greek cabarets along with another friend of ours, Sidi Hassan.

Hassan was a Black Muslim, wore a fez and looked like a Sudanese dervish. He'd been born in South Carolina from an Afro-American family and was connected with an Afro-American cultural organization. He was wise, gentle and philosophical, but he became deadly when angered or insulted.

Hassan was vehemently anti-Christian. He and Sudić would have been sworn enemies in a former age and place, but here, in Canada, with a common enemy in the Anglo-Canadian babblers of the Canadian myth, they followed a sort of armed truce. Like Sudić had said, "Even the Serbs and the Turks united to repel an invasion from Bulgaria."

I was a middle man. Gypsies had fought on both sides in these Balkan wars while the majority stayed out of the fighting altogether. Since I was an anti-religionist, both men considered me their friend.

One evening towards the end of March the three of us were sitting in my place listening to some music that Sudić had borrowed from a friend. I put on one of the records, the music of the Pathans, a warrior hill clan from the North of India, related to the Gypsies. It was savage, martial stuff, the type of music we liked. I saw my friends' faces change as they listened to it. I had a collection of weapons and other curios hanging on the walls of my study. Like most rootless people who aspire to higher status, I had tried to buy myself a past, although Arabian scimitars, *Gurkha kukris*, North-African flintlocks and Hindu daggers were hardly Canadiana.

To go with the music I had a Pathan rifle, a single shot Martini Enfield of Kipling fame, the type of thing they manufactured, copying a captured original, up in the hills in hidden factories.

I pointed it out to the boys and their eyes gleamed. Sudić got up, grabbed it from the wall and started dancing wildly in time to the music.

"*Živela Srbija*," he yelled, "*Smrt u Seldžuki*—Long live Serbia. Death to the Turks!"

Hassan pulled a curved scimitar from the opposite wall and joined him. "*Allah*," he shouted, "*Allah akhbar*—Death to the infidels!"

He started following Sudić in a circle as the Serb held the rifle over his head with both hands and Hassan struck the barrel with the flat of the scimitar. I looked at my tapestry on the wall. It showed two young Turkish warriors wearing their national costumes dancing on a small mat. One had a curved sword, the other a matchlock musket, with a curved stock. Young men were sitting on the ground around them playing drums and flutes while old men were smoking Turkish pipes and probably thinking of their own valiant youth. Women stood off to one side and a mosque loomed in the background.

"Christ," I thought, "I'm seeing the past. What the hell are these two guys doing in Canada? Waiting for a holy way?"

Marie came up the hallway and stood in the doorway with Delilah, my oldest daughter.

"Yanko," she said. "Stop them before they hurt each other."

"They're only doing a war dance."

Delilah, who was six now, stood there watching them. Poor kid, I thought, she's growing up in a virile world surrounded by savages and warriors, Gypsies, Indians, Black Muslims and Serbian *hajduks*, but by the time she's old enough to get married, there won't be any real men like us left. We're a dying breed. Soon the plastic people will rule the world.

The boys became more warlike, screaming their respective and opposing battle cries. Hassan started twirling, wildly, like a dervish, making bold swipes with the scimitar, almost beheading my statue of the kneeling flower girl on the end table. The record came to an end and they stopped dancing just as the doorbell rang. They collapsed into the two armchairs as I went to open the door. It was Pavlos with the expression of a man who has just received a sentence of death. He came in quietly and sat down.

"What happened?" I asked him. "You look terrible."

"I've been wiped out. My studio, cameras, everything, it's gone."

He started his story. He'd owed a fair amount of money and he'd been told to pay up or else. So he'd gone into commercial photography and then ran up an impressive collection of parking tickets on his economy-line van which he'd left parked all over hell's creation while he was working. The police had paid him a visit and told him to pay off the tickets, right away, or be their guest for fifteen days. He didn't have the money so he spent two weeks in jail. He no sooner returned to his studio than a bailiff showed up with a court order and seized everything of value. His van, meanwhile, was in the municipal pound where it had been towed as an abandoned vehicle the same day he'd been arrested.

His magazine had been a big flop, his nude exhibition hadn't materialized and the man who might have had the influence with the Greek pavilion at Expo had been arrested for rape.

His only hope now was to start again in another city out west.

"Can I leave my personal things with you, Yanko?" he asked.

I told him he was welcome to and we'd pick them up right away with Hassan's station wagon.

We brought his stuff back and I told him he could stay with me until he left town.

"I feel terrible," he said. "Crucified, destroyed, ravished by society." He knew English well but always translated literally from Greek.

"Let's go to the Greek club," Sudić suggested. He was sensitive enough to feel the guy's sorrow.

Pavlos agreed. Greeks when they are happy, sad, angry or frustrated usually express themselves by singing, dancing or punching. We went over to the Greek club on St. Lawrence near Rachel and took a table. It wasn't very crowded, but there was a show. I gave Pavlos ten dollars in small bills, but he didn't feel much like dancing. Sudić got onto the stage, asked the orchestra for a Serbian butcher's dance, then did the wild *hasapikos* accompanied by loud yells and heavy thuds.

Pavlos drank *uzo* and sang sad songs in Greek to the music of the orchestra. He looked funny, pathetic and hopeless. He'd never succeed in Canada anymore than I would. Finally, he got up onto the stage and threw a couple of dollars to the orchestra, after asking them for a special dance. Then he did the number, a sad, slow dance. Accompanied by the wailing notes of the Greek clarinet, he fell to his knees, slapped the floor with his hands, then leapt high into the air like a fledgling eagle. It was the dance of a man trying to free himself from the fetters of banal, earthly existence and to reunite himself with the realm of the spiritual, to reach the sacred temples of his gods. I saw the rip suddenly appear in his trousers as his old black suit gave way under the muscular motions of his body. He must have worn out all of his underwear, I thought, as his bare backside became visible through the large tear. The audience must have seen it too, but nobody laughed. They were Greeks. He finished his dance and returned to the table, went to sit down, then realized what had happened.

"Yanko," he said sadly, "even my last pair of pants is gone."

Soon the belly dancer came onto the stage and did her routine. She was a wild, oriental, and had long black hair. She wore an authentic North-African costume and Hassan watched her, fascinated, but not in a sexual way; he seemed hypnotized.

Sudić probably saw her as part of his non-existant harem while Pavlos must have thirsted to get her in front of his camera. She rolled on the floor in time to the music, flashing her black thighs and her African beauty. The dance finished; she left the stage passing near our table. Hassan got up and spoke to her in Gullah for a few seconds.

"Where's she from?" I asked him when he came back. "Tunis, Cairo, Khartoum?"

He shook his head. "South Carolina," he said. "I used to go to school with her."

"What a world," I thought. An Afro-American dancer doing a show in a Greek cabaret in French Montreal. In my hometown, anything is possible.

About a week later the three of us were sitting in the same club when Jilko walked in. He looked furtive and dangerous.

"Jilko," I called to him, "for Christ's sake! Why didn't you come around to see Marie and me?" I asked him. "I heard you got out of jail. All the Gypsies know where I live."

"Yanko," he said. "I know where you live but I no come. You big shot now, is better you not know Jilko."

"You're my friend."

"Ve all friends lonk time ago. Now is everything different."

"What are you doing?" I asked him. "There's a lot of openings over at Expo for violinists like you in the cabarets and restaurants. We could get you in there. What do you think, Draža?"

"Sure," Sudić replied, slapping Jilko on the back. "There's lots of openings, maybe in the Koliba. I'll ask around."

"Is no good, Yanko," Jilko told me. "I no more play music."

"But you're good," I argued. "I still have your violin at home, I kept it for you, even though we were starving sometimes."

He smiled sadly. "You keep, Yanko. Is good *lavuta*. You keep and remember Jilko. Maybe is one day your son play like Jilko. Me, I no more play."

"Oh, come on. You'll forget about the prison. We'll get you some phony papers, you can change your identity."

Suddenly he thrust both hands over the table. We all stared, shocked. The fingers had been broken and hadn't been set properly. He'd never play anything but a jukebox or a record player as long as he lived.

"What happened?" I asked him.

"Police is do this. Is big riot in St. Vincent de Paul. Everybody fight, men killed, guards is beat me up, knock me down and put feet on hands."

"*Pička njim materina*," Sudić mouthed a vile Serbian oath.

Hassan said nothing but a sad smile flitted across his eyes.

Pavlos was horrified. "The filthy swine," he said. Those might well have been his hands, he must have realized.

Poor Jilko. Now he was totally unemployable.

"What will you do now?" I asked him wondering if we could get him a job as a waiter or something at Expo.

"I steal," he said simply.

Yes, I realized, that's about all he really had left now. To become part of a gang of Hungarian immigrants who prowled around the city smashing store windows, stealing watches and pimping for their women, even sticking up banks or mugging drunks on the weekend. One day, I knew, he'd lie dead in some garbage-littered alleyway with a slug in his back or get sent up for life. I remembered my boss: "Some animals can't survive outside their natural habitat."

Jilko opened his jacket and showed us the revolver in the shoulder holster.

"This time police is no catch Jilko," he said. "This time I kill police."

22

The opening day of Expo was chaos. I got down to the exhibition early only to find that our stuffed caribou hadn't arrived. Its case was ready and its natural habitat was piled up nearby, but the beast itself was somewhere between Montreal and Calgary.

Smith had dismissed all the workers except three. He and I would run the exhibit in shifts; we had a bunch of miniskirted girls to show people around and two older, uglier, but more competent, women to run the souvenir stands. We also had a couple of Indians dressed up in feathers and buckskin, Charlie and Joseph. They were guides and trappers and they had a miniature encampment in the exhibit. Apparently the boss had decided to include them among the rest of the animals even though they weren't stuffed. I wondered if one of them should get sick or need first aid whether to call the Expo medical service or the S.P.C.A.

Steadman rushed in right after me.

"Where's the elk?" he asked, looking at the empty showcase.

"Caribou," I corrected him.

He grabbed the phone and called the C.P.R.

"Where's our moose?" he asked them. "There's been a bugger-up somewhere."

He finally got through to somebody who knew where it was.

"It's in the station," he told us. "We'll have to go and pick it up. All their trucks are busy."

I called Joseph, the Indian, over to the only truck we had.

"Will a large caribou fit in there?" I asked him.

He shrugged his shoulders. "I see some, fit for sure; I see some, no fit; I see some more, maybe fit."

Christ, I thought, some help he is. Why the hell didn't they send the damned thing alive? We could have knocked it off and stuffed it here. We all went to the station and found it standing in a shed. What a monster! We hoisted it into the truck with the aid of a crane and the help of an army of railroad employees, then lashed it firmly in position with ropes.

"I guess this calls for a drink, men," Steadman told us and we all piled into the back of the truck with the caribou, and he got in the front with the driver and Smith.

He bought a case of beer and a bottle of scotch for himself on the way back and we drank the beers as the driver tried to get through the mass of traffic heading for Expo. It was tough going but we finally made it through the milling crowds waiting to get in, only to find that the caribou wouldn't go through the door of the exhibit building. Even Smith hadn't thought of that, but he was undaunted.

"Get to work, you guys," he yelled at the three labourers. "Smash that fucking door frame wider and higher so we can get this sonofabitch inside. I'll get some more boys over from headquarters later to build it up again."

The three workmen, Smith, the Indians and I got to work with crowbars, axes and mallets. Once the doorway was demolished we finally got the thing inside with the help of about fifty Expo employees, security guards, Montreal cops and unidentifiable lookers-on. But now, another problem arose.

"For Christ's sake," Smith said, "it's too high to go into the showcase. The antlers are sticking up about six inches too much."

But Smith was a man used to doing the impossible.

"Joe," he yelled to a labourer. "Bring me a stepladder and a hacksaw." He set up the stepladder on one side of the specimen, climbed up it and started sawing off a fair sized chunk of the antlers. It fell with a thud.

"That should fix up this side," he said, as he climbed down the ladder. He repeated his mutilation on the other side and came back down the ladder again to get a rasp.

"Now I'll just rasp 'em back to look normal."

He rasped away as Steadman hopped from side to side at the bottom of the ladder.

"The boss must never know about this," he told Smith. "He'd be heartbroken. It only beat the Edmonton entry by six inches. It's not the biggest in Canada anymore."

"What the hell, Steadman," Smith yelled back. "We gotta open today. Who the hell's gonna get in there to measure it."

The place was a real mess now with the doorway smashed and the floor littered with debris. We were all filthy and the Indians had ruined their feathers and torn their Japanese buckskins.

Smith grabbed the phone.

"Hello, MacIntosh," he yelled, "get a gang over on the double. We gotta build a new doorway, plaster it up and fix the place. Expo's gonna be open in about ten minutes."

After the episode of the caribou, things went fairly smoothly during the Expo. Only two other problems arose and Smith rose to meet them also. We'd received numerous manikins for our displays but they were almost all females. Smith solved that one easily.

"We'll just smash the tits off and do something with the arms. The heads can be done back at the headquarters."

A final problem emerged a month after opening when some zoologist pointed out in a letter to the editor of the Montreal Star that our male and female specimens of some deer or other were actually two males.

Smith, when informed, drew his hunting knife.

"Off with its balls," he said. "The sonofabitch got no antlers."

Towards the end of the season Bill dropped over to see me.

"Think you can stick it out, Yanko?" he asked me as we sat in the room Smith and I were using as a combination office-workshop.

"No," I said, "it's no use. I've spoken to all kinds of people. Nobody's interested in me or my ships. I'm thinking of going over to Europe where ship model building is considered an art."

"But you're a Canadian, Yanko."

"Any shmuck who is born here is a Canadian," I told him, remembering Alec, "but you have to be a Wasp to claim your birthright."

"Where will you go?" he asked.

"Probably England first. I could try the museums there, they've got enough of them. If not, maybe France."

"And what if you don't get anything there?" he asked.

"I'll get rid of all this junk I've been carrying around for years and just be one more Gypsy. My wife can tell fortunes."

"But the money's good here," he said.

I rattled the keys on my belt. "Sure the money's good but I'm nothing but a fucking watchman. I'm not accepted for what I can do;

I'm just a pawn of these rich condescending pricks who've decided on a personal whim that I should be here. One guy with his tobacco factory poisoning people to death, another with his brewery rotting their guts away, they control the arts in this country, the Canada Council, everything. They're always screaming about the fact that there's no Canadian culture but they keep on blocking anybody who has something serious to offer. Why? Because once they allow a true Canadian culture to emerge they'll become as extinct as the dodo."

"Well, good luck," Bill said. "Me, I'll stay and fight. The bastards won't chase me out of my own country. They'll have to bury me first."

"They just might," I said, getting a mental picture of Tom Smith acting as temporary gravedigger and his probable comment: "What the boss wants, we keep, what he don't want, we get rid of."

Bill left and when Smith came in to replace me for the late shift I went over to the Swiss Hut.

A young hippie joined me.

"You're a Gypsy, aren't you?" he asked.

"I am," I told him. "Why?"

"Your *copain* is sick over in the house where I'm living. He's asked us to look for you here."

We went to an old house on Clark Street above Sherbrooke where I found Kolia lying on a filthy bed in a room littered with clothes, garbage and junk of all sorts.

"Yanko," he said. "I knew you'd come. I'm sick."

He had a high fever, so I went to a nearby restaurant and called the doctor. At first he didn't want to come, but I assured him I'd pay cash. He gave Kolia an injection, told me he'd be all right and left after I paid him.

Kolia looked much older, very tired and had streaks of grey in his hair.

"Yanko," he told me, "get out of this country. The devil is on the earth here. In this room, I could have died like a dog, without candles, *pomana* feast, nothing, and my soul would have wandered eternally in the darkness of *Kalisferia*. I'll get back to Europe somehow. If I must die, I'll die among the Roms. Come over and I'll show you the Kalderash camps around Paris, the *Gitanos Canasteros* in Spain, the Sinti in Italy. Our people here are finished. They'll all die in the cities along with the *Gazhe*."

"*Si tu pasaporto?*" I asked him.

"Yes, I have one, Canadian," he told me.

I looked at him, remembering the past. Through him I'd met the Gypsies, Marie, the old man. I'd seen many things and I'd found myself, which was something, even if I hadn't succeeded in my work. I'd failed and I knew why. Certain factors are inescapable, but, because of Kolia, I was no longer angry.

"There is not to love, nor to hate, there is only to understand." That's a Romani saying. I wanted to add: "and perhaps to feel a little sad." Perhaps, after all, we Gypsies really were the bastard sons of Abraham and Hagar, the Egyptian, cursed to roam the world as pariahs with every man's hand against us to fulfil the prophecy of the Ishmaelites, who many erudite Biblical scholars believe to be not the Arabs but the Children of Roma once called "Egyptians" and now corrupted to "Gypsy".

I wrote Kolia a cheque, enough for his passage back to France.

"*Zha Devlesa*," I told him. "Go with God."

He didn't give me the formal Gypsy reply "Stay with God." Instead, he took my hand.

"You know, don't you, Yanko?"

"Yes, Kolia, I know. You tried with Tinka, but it wouldn't work. But it's not a sin. It's just that the Gypsies don't understand these things. Take a man like Charlie, he loves women, yes, but what is he? You worked, you followed your laws, you supported the old people, you've never injured anybody. You knew I chose women and you never bothered me."

"Good luck, Yanko," he said, "and say goodby to Marie and your children for me."

Not many of the regular gang were in the Honest John, a new hangout we had taken to going to. It was run by two British ex-mercenaries who'd made a pile of money in some African war and used it to open this English-style pub in Montreal.

I joined a small group of Canadian Indians I knew. One of them was taking a course in dramatic art, a would-be actor. He hadn't made anything big yet, like Johnny Yesno on "Wojek", but he had his aspirations. The Indians discussed their problems. They were the ones who'd shown promise in the mission schools and had now been brought to the city to attend university. The whole idea was to teach them trades and professions that would be useless back where they came from, forcing them to settle in urban centres where it was hoped, they would intermarry, assimilate and lose their rights and identities as Indians. Their children, born in the cities, would be classified as *Métis*. The dummies back on the reservations would be given free birth control pills and the Indian problem might be easily solved as the depopulated reservations were sold to private speculators.

Many of these kids drank heavily, a few did dope. Older families of Indian tradesmen and their wives served as a basis for their society and tried to help the youngsters. But the older Indians were in many cases barely literate and couldn't understand these university-educated youngsters.

My actor friend was happy. He'd just received and signed a contract to appear in some western series for a substantial figure. He'd never thought of himself earning so much money. But he was also a virulent spokesman for his people and could see through the nauseating policy of "brotherhood" crapped out by Ottawa. He knew that he'd be appearing in a stereotype production propagating the same old gut-wrenching hogwash.

He told me how his father, a trapper, seldom made over three hundred dollars a year and how most of this went right back to the Hudson Bay Company for supplies and luxuries like soap, matches and ammunition to shoot more animals with. The company sold the rifles, the traps, the ammunition, the food, clothing and everything else. They bought the pelts and they set the prices. If somebody complained too loudly, they called in the R.C.M.P.

Sally, a Cree barfly, joined us. She and her roommate smoked pot. They hung out in the Honest John conning the young white executives out of drinks by giving them the false impression that they had willing red sex to offer. They never came across but sneaked out the back door just before closing time, leaving their benefactor for the evening with a hard on and a pair of lover's nuts.

The others drifted off until only the actor, Sally and I remained. He'd passed out, stoned out of his mind. He had his contract in his pocket, but he was already trying to lose himself in the oblivion of a bottle. What would he be like after six months of acting the role of a stereotype Tonto?

"I'd better take him home," I said to Sally.

Sally helped me to get him out. He puked a few times as Sally ran up the road to flag down a hack. I manhandled him into the back seat, then got in front with the driver. Sally went back to the club.

He lived with a group of students in the house of Indian Johnnie, the welder, and his wife not far away. I tried to bring him around, but it was useless. He kept mumbling in his drunken stupor: "My name, an offense; my Christian name, humiliation; my status, a rebel; my age, the stone age."

Christ, the guy was quoting Fanon's bible of the oppressed.

We got to his place, I opened the door to get him out just as he puked all over the back seat.

"*Sacrement!*" the driver exploded. "Get that drunken savage out of there."

I slipped him a few bucks to cover the cleaning costs and got my friend upstairs.

Johnnie and his wife answered the buzzer, took a fast look and summed up what had happened.

"Let's get him inside," Johnnie said, unexcited.

The three of us carried him into his bedroom and placed him on the mattress on the floor.

Then we went into the living room.

"Want a drink, Yanko?" Johnnie asked as we heard the war-cries and the guns firing on T.V. The Indians fled before the charging cavalry.

"Jesus Christ, we're losing again," Johnnie yelled to his wife. "Shut that fucking thing off Annie before I put my stinking foot through it."

We had a couple as the actor moaned in the bedroom.

"He drinks too much," Johnnie said. "We all drink, but some of the boys can't hold their liquor. We Indian people don't belong here in the city. Me, I stay, I'm a welder, get good money and all that. But Annie here wants to go back. She misses her folks and the old things. But it's like I keep telling her: What the fuck is there to do there? These young guys, like him, they're funny though. They get soft jobs like pulling teeth or working for the Government, but they're always complaining. Me I gotta freeze my nuts off on construction jobs, sixty feet up in the air. One bad step and down you go."

"I'd better go see to him," Johnnie's wife said as the actor's moaning grew suddenly more agonized.

"Christ," she yelled from the bedroom. "He's just shit himself. Jesus, what a mess."

"No, we don't belong here," Johnnie said again, opening another beer.

He poured me a glass, then raised his own in a toast.

"*Shnegiraguh,*" he said, "You heard of Red Power, Yanko?"

"*Ni-i harashkarageghta ni-ogwehunkweh,*" I replied, "I stand as one with the Iroquois nation."

"I forgot," he said. "But they'll see. We're fighters. They'll have trouble soon. Already we're holding meetings and a lot of the boys got guns. They all know how to use 'em. That's the good thing about being a reservation-born Indian. We all know how to shoot. Sure, they can teach us all that Jesus crap, hymns and prayers and other shit, but they can't stop us from learning how to shoot. Anyway, it's better to die with a gun in your hand than as a lush on Skid Row with a bottle of whisky. What do you think?"

His wife passed carrying a bowl of water and some cloths. I could smell the horrible stench from the bedroom.

"Yes," I agreed, "or in your own puke and shit like that poor guy in there."

"Your wife's one of us," he went on, "you speak some of our lingo and hang around with us. You ain't no white man, why don't you come with us? Red Power, that's the answer, we'll show the bastards."

I glanced at the hunting rifle on his wall, polished and oiled, the weapon of a trained hunter and I got visions of Johnnie and his people someday up in the bush where nobody could get at them except on foot, and shooting the boss's beloved animals for food and through sabotage, sniping, guerrilla warfare, poisoning reservoirs, burning down timber reserves costing our Government millions to control. Three hundred warriors among a population of thousands of innocent trappers, hunters and farmers. Who were they, where were they?

"No, Johnnie," I told him. "When I fight, it'll be the Gypsy way."

"What way's that, Yanko?"

But I had no answer to give him.

E Zor Devleski, or the power of the universal intellect, shows that whatever man may build, the power of intellect can destroy. Man must never usurp the role of God and try to interfere with the natural order of things. The tower can be built on the bodies of the slaves but one day the lightening will strike and the tower will fall, spilling the arrogant master to his doom among the filth and misery that he has created.

This is where Yanko realizes that truth.

— 23 —

I gave my notice to the boss. I would finish out the season, take a week's rest and then throw one last party before leaving the following Friday. It was Saturday night and I wanted to pay one last visit to all the hangouts in a ceremony of farewell. I wanted to see again, probably for the last time, the city and all the places where I had sat and talked for the last ten years, to remember the past.

Marie came with me, wearing her Mexican-type dress, white blouse, embroidered bodice and a pair of leather knee-high boots. Her long hair was combed out in the Gypsy style. Somehow, she always managed to look like both a Gypsy and an Indian at the same time. She had learned to speak fairly good *Romanes* and was as good a fortuneteller as the other women. I wore the fringed and beaded cowskin jacket she had made me under my sportscoat and had my bowie knife with the beaded sheath, her Christmas present, inside my boot as usual.

We went first to the Swiss Hut. It was now the hangout of motorcycle gangs, petty hoods and hippies.

Our next stop was El Cortijo. It too had changed. It was now a separatist stronghold and it was there that the first radical separatist publication, *La Forge*, had been published by young, would-be revolutionaries who were now making a name for themselves in politics. I met many of my French-Canadian artist friends there, people we had known back in the old days, intellectuals who had laughed, drunk and sung with us. They were serious now, the time for jokes was over. We saw the depths of hatred and resentment that would soon explode.

We left El Cortijo and walked over to St. Lawrence Boulevard, turning down towards St. Catherine Street. This too had changed. There were no more wide-open Gypsy fortunetelling stores, no brothels. The vice was still here but the Mafia had moved in. Everything was organized and controlled with a minimum of violence.

We walked along St. Catherine Street amid the noise and bustle. The air felt heavy and ominous, as if the wrath of God or man would strike soon. I thought of all the poverty in the world and here in Canada, and I knew that these evil cities couldn't last for long. All the affluence, bright lights, banality and carnalism amid the squalor of the slums.

Showtime, showtime, lots of girls; honk-honk; Watch your step buddy, who the fuck are you pushing; Vive le Québec libre; Law and order, more law and order; Our youth must be brought back to Christ; We must preserve our wildlife at all costs. The slogans and the madness amid the glittering lights and commercialized sex were overpowering.

We made our way to the Bistro and found Bill sitting there as usual. We joined him and I told him that this was our last trip around the hangouts. I'd just received my passport and I glanced through it, looking at the clauses and instructions for Canadians planning to reside abroad. A friend of ours came in and joined us.

"Christ," he informed us, "the separatists just blew up the public toilet in the bus terminal. A guy was killed and some others were taken away in an ambulance."

I glanced at notice five in my passport, which related to Canadians who might get into difficulties in a foreign country: *"Changes of address or departure from the country should be notified. Registration helps Canadian authorities to assist Canadian citizens in an emergency."*

What a joke, I thought, the Federal Government can't even guarantee your safety in a public shithouse in Montreal. What do they figure to do in Spain or the Belgian Congo?

Bill, Marie and I left the Bistro and walked over to the Honest John. There was a mob standing outside, office girls with their boyfriends, squares, middle class junior executives and pseudo-hippies. All the hard-working, myth-swallowing creations of the system had come down to see the kooks, the oddballs, the fairies, the Indians and the crackpots, just like people used to do in Victorian England when they would spend the afternoon in the lunatic asylum watching and goading the inmates for entertainment. I noticed that many of the mob were regulars, Blacks, Indians, hippies and student agitators.

"They won't let us in," Johnnie the Indian welder told us, "Indian George got thrown out last week and they're afraid we might start trouble. These rich weekend people spend a lot more than we do. We drink only beer and wine."

"What?" Bill snarled. "They won't keep us out tonight. Yanko here is leaving and this is his last night out with his wife. Listen you guys, I have a plan."

Bill suddenly changed. He became serious, organized, a leader of men. He told the regulars to get away from the door and gather in the lane around the corner where there was a stairway leading up into the washroom of the Honest John.

"I'll get in with Yanko," he told them, "then we'll open the door of the shithouse and let you guys in."

The regulars took off and vanished around the corner.

"Come on, Yanko," Bill told me. "We're going in."

I looked at Marie. She smiled. "I'll go into the lane with the rest of the natives. See you later."

Bill walked up to the door, pushing his way angrily through the mob and thumped on the door with his big fist. He looked like a typical English Canadian, well dressed and seemingly a respectable member of contemporary Wasp society. The waiter guarding the door opened it. He was letting in a select number of the more prosperous-looking weekenders.

"Sorry, filled up," he told Bill.

Bill said, "Oh, I just ate here and left my umbrella. May I get it?"

"Certainly, Sir," the waiter said.

Bill strode inside and I tried to follow.

"Not you, Mister," the waiter grabbed my arm.

I pulled out my Expo identity card and flashed it in front of him, fast.

"I'm sorry, sir," he apologized, and I walked in.

The place was really crowded and the usual crowd had come early; George, Sudić, Hassan, Etien the separatist, and many more including a fair number of Indians, I saw Charlie and Joseph from the exhibit. Bill had vanished upstairs and I walked over to George who was sitting at a table full of young girls.

"Got that pilot issue with the article you did on me?" I asked him.

He'd just done a story on me and the pilot issue was due out three weeks before the article actually appeared. He handed it to me. He had taken his usual colourful approach. I'd be lucky to get a job washing dishes in Canada after this thing was published. Yanko, the drunken hard-fisted Gypsy intellectual stood portrayed in all of his barbaric sensitivity.

"How do you like it, Yanko?" George grinned. He was obviously proud of his story. What could I tell him? You can't hate a fool.

I went upstairs to see what Bill was doing. I found him struggling with the door, kicking at it in a clumsy, frustrated attempt to open it.

"Can you open this thing, Yanko?" he asked.

I smiled, took out some special keys and in a second it was open.

"Good man," he smiled. "We could use guys like you in the revolution. Too bad you're leaving."

The crowd started climbing the stairs, Marie at their head, Indians, Blacks, hippies, new lefters, artists and other outcasts.

"Come on, you guys," Bill yelled at them. "The pigs won't keep us out if we want to get in. Down with the exploiting bastards. Long live the Canadian revolution."

The mob surged up the stairs, into the bathroom and out onto the landing leading downstairs. I don't think any of them were thinking about revolutions: it was Saturday night. Marie joined Bill and me and we followed them down. The waiters tried valiantly to stem the invasion but it was hopeless. Like a herd of inflamed stallions rushing towards their waiting mares they swarmed past the waiters in their headlong charge. The Indians, some already half-stoned, rushed over to the front door and opened it. "Come on in," Indian Charlie yelled. "Let's have a shindig."

Now another mob of invaders surged in from the street outside and soon the place was so crowded that it became almost impossible to move. The waiters tried to eject the obvious intruders, but it was almost impossible to say who had forced their way in and who had been there in the first place. They refused to serve some people they recognized as gate crashers and these guys started swiping bottles of beer from the tables of the customers and bothering their women. Arguments started and I saw one black guy struggling with a waiter. The band stopped playing and it looked like there might be trouble. One of the English owners rushed over to the jukebox and put some change into it. He must have figured the music would make the people start dancing. It didn't. I edged over to where Sudić and Hassan were standing. If there was going to be a rumble, I wanted to be alongside them. Sudić was a powerful giant and Hassan was fast and deadly, a karate expert. As I took Marie's hand to lead her over I suddenly saw Cherie. Christ, I thought, I'm glad Marie never saw her, or had she. Anyway, it was quite a while since I'd had my affair with her.

"It looks like trouble," I told my friends.

"*Dobro,*" Sudić grinned punching the flat of his left palm with his fist. He was always looking for somebody to replace the non-existant Turks. Tonight he would be quite happy to settle for Wasps.

I saw Bill get onto the stage and grab the microphone. The Black band just sat there, silent. They all knew him. His powerful voice boomed across the pub compelling the mob to silence; some hippie girl turned down the volume of the jukebox. I saw George sitting in the corner with a quart bottle of beer in his hand. He looked sad, dejected and half-stoned. The pilot issue of the magazine lay on the table beside him.

"Listen you guys," Bill yelled. "Why do you take shit from these arrogant Limey piglets who make money by killing African patriots to come here and open a fucking pub. The bastards can't keep us out if we want to get in. We're Canadians, our money is as good as theirs. What's the matter with you dummies. Don't stand there giggling like a bunch of schoolgirls grateful that they finally let you in. You Indians, Blacks, socialists, hippies and thinkers, they call you whores, dogs, savages and crackpots. Why do you eat their shit? Fight back you cunts, you're Canadians, this is your country as well. Down with the pigs and their pig trough! Long live the Canadian revolution!"

"Fuck off, you stupid drunk," a weekender yelled.

"Drunk?" Bill replied. "Listen you arsehole. I'm not an ordinary drunk, I'm a socialist revolutionary, you fascist Turdeau-loving pigs."

Somebody threw a bottle at Bill, he ducked and it smashed against the wall behind him, splattering the Black band with fragments of glass. They mumbled ominously.

"Communist," another guy yelled, "stinking red bastard."

"We got freedom," another added, "this is Canada."

"Sure we got freedom," Bill screamed back. "But it's for sale like everything else. We sell freedom, women, cars, pornography, hot dogs, gimmicks and garbage; you name it buddy, and we got it, and with the right connections you can get it wholesale."

Bill grabbed the Canadian flag from the wall nearby where it hung along with the Union Jack and the Stars and Stripes, ripped off the last two thirds and left only the first part, the red flag of socialism.

"I'm no Communist," he yelled at his hecklers. "You filthy rotten scum. I'm a Canadian, a patriot, a socialist. You pigs work for the puppet-masters and eat their shit. Wake up you fools. Give the Indian back his pride, give the Black man equality, give the people intelligent leadership and make this country a better place to live in and raise a family, force them to open the doors and let in the immigrants we need to build up this country so we can tell the Yanks to fuck off. You Indians, Blacks, socialists and thinkers, how long are you gonna stand for this bullshit. Wake up you sonovabitches and fight. Forward with the red flag."

"I'm for that," Johnnie the Indian welder cried. "Red flag for Red Power, *Harraaskwah.*" The Mohawk battle cry rang out as he threw a full bottle of beer at the table where Bill's antagonists were sitting. It smashed on the wall above them, showering them with glass and beer. Other Indians answered his warcry. Christ, I thought as I pulled Marie behind me, this is it.

"Looks like Custer's gonna get it again," she smiled.

Some guy threw a glass at Indian Johnnie who was standing out in the open daring all comers. It missed him and hit the wall showering one of the Black Panthers with glass. He was one of a bunch that had come up for the weekend from New York to get away from the racial tension for a while. He took his hands away from his face and stared at the open bloody palms for a second, his face contorted into a diabolical look of hatred.

"Brothers," he screamed to his friends. "Let's get them white mother-fuckers." The brawl erupted as the Panthers charged the table of about twenty well-dressed office types who had been deriding Bill. Their faces showed terror as the Blacks closed in.

"*Živela Srbija,*" Sudić bellowed, flattening some guy with one blow and grabbing another. Everybody chose which side he was on. There was a common hatred and a common enemy, but each fighter had his own reasons for fighting. Sudić knocked guys down like a blast of shrapnel. He was back on some ancient battlefield, maybe Kosovo. These were Turks, despoilers of the sacred soil of Holy Serbia. Hassan, near him was fighting an old war of liberation, "*Allah,*" he kept shouting as he rabbit punched and booted his opponents, "*Allah,* you white mother-fuckers."

I fought as best I could, trying to defend myself and Marie at the same time. I remembered Jilko, Kolia, the old man, Pavlos, and how we had put our first baby girl in a cardboard box on top of a bureau so the rats couldn't get at her until she was old enough not to be smothered by the cats we bought to protect her. All the rejection, the suffering, the ridicule and the inability of those in power to understand our problems. It was all here, concentrated in these babblers of the Canadian myth, these ignorant fools who condemned people to misery and suffering because they were too bloody stupid to wake up and analyze what was going on. They kept on voting for the same worthless politicians year after year, Tweedle Dum and Tweedle Dee. They were nothing but sheep, well-paid lackeys of the system they perpetrated by their apathetic disinterest. They couldn't care less what went on in Canada so long as they were O.K.

"*Kurav tumare Devlen,*" I screamed in *Romanes,* as I booted some Germanic-looking characters in the nuts, "I defile your Gods." He crumpled and I gave him a Judo chop over the left ear, "for Jilko," I added, as I ground his hands into the stone floor with my boot. "You stupid *Gazho* pig."

All the pent up hatreds of these oppressed minority groups and individuals were exploding right here and the weekenders were scared shitless. They had no real cause to fight for and their main thought was to defend themselves or to escape. Women fell and were trampled on and Black, Indian and artist girls grappled with the sexy dates of the weekenders, ripping their clothes or pulling their hair. Many of our girls were throwing bottles at the bar, smashing the mirrors and the bottles lined up there for sale. Somebody turned up the jukebox and the music of "Black Day in July" played above the noise of the fight.

I saw Joe, the drifter, struggling with a much smaller executive type. His common-law wife, Margo, was helping him, pounding his smaller opponent with her heavy handbag and yelling at him. "Leave him alone, leave him alone, you big bully."

"Yahoo," the Indian warcries were continuous. I was glad they were on my side as I saw them, mostly small light guys, take a terrific pounding from some heavier opponent just to get in close enough to grapple. Once they did, he was finished. Some big guy grabbed me and we fell to the floor. He was much too strong for me and I tried to reach down to my boot to get at the razor sharp bowie knife.

"*Jebem ti pizdu materinu,*" I heard a familiar voice explode and the guy suddenly vanished as Sudić picked him up and threw him away like a child hurling his teddy bear while having a tantrum. He crashed into a table covered with bottles and the whole thing went down underneath him, the bottles rolling on the floor. "*Za krst časni i slobodu zlatnu,*" Sudić bellowed, "For the holy cross and glorious freedom."

He stood there, his eyes searching for another opponent as the bottles fell against him and bounced off again.

A powerfully built man went for Hassan, looming over him, ready to grind him into a pulp. "You dumb nigger," he yelled.

"*Allah,*" Hassan replied as he went into a crouch, slipped under the guy's crotch, stood up and felled him from behind. The guy went down and stayed down.

"*Allah* is victorious," Hassan called to me in triumph.

I rushed madly into a knot of weekenders, grabbed some guy about my own size, slammed him against the wall and drew back my first to smash his teeth in. But I held my punch. It was my half-brother.

"Get out," I told him. "This way, by the back stairs." I pushed him over to the stairs. "We're on different sides now kid, this is civil war. Fight your own battles from now on."

I left him there and returned to the conflict. Somebody had knocked down Joseph from the exhibition and was kneeling over him slugging him in the face. I went over to help him, but before I could get there his wife had jumped the guy and bitten him on the ear. He rolled off in pain and Joseph got up and finished him off with a good boot in the head.

I saw Marie over near the jukebox. She was walking calmly among the struggling fighters, looking for somebody. She kept pushing her way past the fighters, totally unconcerned with the violence around her.

Bill emerged from among the battlers, his clothes were ripped and he had blood on his face. He was smiling and still waving the mutilated Canadian flag.

"Forward men," he yelled. "Victory is in sight. Down with the exploiting swine." He slugged some guy over the head with the flagpole and the guy went down like a slaughtered steer. "Forward, men," he yelled again. "Long live the Canadian revolution."

A Canadian Black from Halifax went savagely for a suave Negro spokesman of Canada's Black minority.

"You goddamned traitor," he screamed at him, as he slugged him in the face. "You was born on the same block I was, you stinking nigger."

Near him, my Indian actor friend was happily pounding the shit out of one of Canada's educated Indian broadcasters who read the weekly scripts given to him by his white masters. "*Ostiskwah*, cunt."

Now the struggle grew more controlled. Bodies covered the floor and the place was wrecked. I saw one of the owners laid out near the jukebox, the other was struggling with a huge African student and getting the worst of the fight. The Indians had formed into a compact group, they had a few injured, and their women were attending to them. The Blacks had gathered around the stage to protect their soul brothers in the band, the Black Panthers brandished chains, broken bottles, belts and knives, nobody bothered much with them. Bill was singing loudly and throwing bottles at what was left of the bar, "And over lines of martyred dead, we'll keep the red flag flying high." He was singing some socialist anthem.

I saw two girls wrestling on the floor, their clothes were ripped and their thighs flashed as they rolled and tore savagely at each other. Even the women were fighting now.

Marie was getting the better of Cherie, whose clothes were almost torn to pieces. They got to their feet and I saw the stiletto glittering in the flickering light of the candles hanging in glass orbs from the ceiling. She slashed at the singer and cut the remains of her clothes from her body as the Indian women laughed and the men whistled or yelled warcries.

"*Ostiskwah*," Marie shouted, as she reduced Cherie to her brassiere, panties and stockings. "*Utkoo*," she yelled again, as she slashed at her garter belt. It fell down to her knees taking her stockings with it. Cherie tripped and fell to the stone floor. Marie lunged again and cut the strings of the brassiere, grabbed it and threw it among the Indians. Cherie yelled for help and some gallant hero tried to stop Marie and Johnnie sent him crashing headfirst into the jukebox. I was too busy laughing to do anything. Finally, Cherie was naked and Marie tried to shepherd her out into the street. But she slipped past her and fled up the stairs to lock herself in the women's washroom. The place was emptying fast now.

"Let's go before the cops get here," Sudić suggested.

I saw George, sitting with a group of terrified girls. Poor George. He had no cause to fight, just colourful articles to write to earn his living. He'd certainly got some good material tonight. The Indians headed for the door.

"Let's go," I told the others and we fought our way out, Sudić leading, Hassan, Marie and I following along with the Indians. Nobody could stop the Serbian Hajduk. The brawl had now erupted into the street and I saw the only two telephones in the place lying outside in the doorway. Now I knew why the police hadn't been called.

The Indians flagged down taxis or escaped on foot, making for some prearranged rendezvous where they could celebrate their skirmish over a few drinks. We got into Hassan's station wagon and started to drive away just as I saw Joseph the Indian and his wife standing in the street.

"Get in," I told them, "before the cops arrive."

"Wait for Charlie," he told me.

I heard a wild Cree warhoop followed by the sound of breaking glass. I turned towards the sound of the noise and saw that the huge picture window with the glass inlay of old John Diefenbaker come crashing into the street. Charlie appeared running like hell and jumped into the back of the car followed by Joseph and his wife.

"What a send-off," I thought, as we passed the police cruisers converging on what was left of the Honest John.

24

It was the day of the last party and I had said my last goodbys to the people at the exhibit. They would soon be tearing it down; the stuffed animals, my paintings and other exhibits were to be shipped out to Edmonton for next year's opening. The boss had bought my collection of animal paintings for a reasonable figure and I had left my ship model collection with a friend of mine who was a dealer in antiques, militaria and works of art. He might be able to sell them, he might not; anyway, I couldn't take them with me. I gave the Pathan rifle to Sudić as a souvenir of our friendship and the scimitar to Hassan.

"You'll read about me someday," he grinned as he fingered the edge of the blade with his thumb. "Some crazy nigger shot waving a sword somewhere."

"I doubt it," I told him.

"*Insh-Allah*," he smiled.

I had received a letter from Pavlos, from Greece. It seems he had left Montreal to go out west and met an English immigrant on the way. They had both decided to head for California where Pavlos was arrested because of his obvious European origin and lack of papers. Since he had never bothered to take out Canadian citizenship—one of those trivial banalities he never got around to—he was deported back to Greece. Once on his native soil he had been put into the Greek army to do his military service.

What a tragedy, I thought. I could never see this gentle, artistic Greek, plunging a bayonet through somebody's guts or mowing guys down with a machine gun. Maybe I'd meet him again someday in Europe.

Smith was sorry to see me leave.

"We're a good team, Lee. Them other guys is always goofin' off somewhere, but you and me work good together. You handle all that egghead stuff like cards and all that crap and I take care of the guys. Too bad you're leavin', you shoulda stuck with the boss. Nobody leaves the boss."

No, it's true, I thought, how many people would leave the boss? But I had to get away from these order-taking morons like Smith and the sycophants like Steadman. Their world made a mockery of the years I had spent in the sweat shops and the junk stores. I had believe, once, that I would get somewhere. Now I knew that there was nowhere for me to go.

What kind of society was it where a man could study, struggle and get nowhere and then, some character like the boss could come along and render all of this meaningless by paying him a big salary to do utterly nothing? Back in the sweatshops, I had perhaps been in danger of losing my hope, my health or my honesty, but here I was in danger of losing much more, my sanity.

The two Indians, Charlie and Joseph, weren't going back to the reservation. They had seen the city. There was no segregation in the bars, at least. Marie felt sorry for them but she knew that now they'd seen the central heating, flush toilets, television, the supermarkets and the liquor commission they would never return to the barren wilderness, to the wooden shacks, wood stoves, outdoor toilets and the constant cold and hunger.

The gang was all excited over the party. I'd fixed up the place with balloons and made a large stencil, "The Last Party," in blue and green letters. It was pinned to the wall with thumbtacks just over my Turkish tapestry that hadn't been packed yet.

The Gypsy boys were coming with their instruments and the rest of our gang had been invited. We set a large table with food and liquor and I made a large bowl of potent Gypsy punch and a smaller bowl of non-alcoholic punch for the women and guys like Hassan who didn't drink.

We had packed most of our stuff now and the trunks were lining the walls of the living room. The guests would have to sit on them as the furniture had almost all gone.

Sudić and Hassan arrived first, just ahead of the Gypsies. Jimmy, the star musician, was a colourful character. He was small and skinny with long sideburns and a wry sense of humour. His younger brother, Mathew was a burly, serious youth and very likable. Steve

Demitro, the mandolin player, was the oldest son of the old man. He was a fine musician, but was now suffering from arthritis and he had trouble playing. I remembered him years ago, playing for the Gypsies. Now, almost crippled, he lamented the passing of an era, the last age of the true Gypsy in Canada. He remembered the travelling life, the carnivals, the open country and, unlike the younger men, he hated the city. The young boys who had never known this former nomadic life, couldn't exist without pool rooms, used car lots and plugs for their amplifiers.

Dula, the singing Gypsy sadist, was also at the party. He seldom spoke *Romanes* and was married to a fat English-Canadian woman who was always complaining about him burning her with cigarette butts and belting the daylights out of her. But all she had to do was leave him. She never did, so I guess they were well mated. Dula was a fine soprano and a good bongo player. He was planning to take over my place after I left. It was a solid old house and the noise from outside hardly penetrated the thick walls. I figured that the screams of his wife being tortured wouldn't disturb the upstairs neighbours too much. Anyway, the guy right above me usually bashed his wife around at least once a week. If they timed it right, their sado-masochistic sessions could overlap. Dula was soft spoken and very jovial with his friends. Everybody considered him a nice guy, except his wife. He'd just bought himself a flashy new American car, the envy of all the Gypsies, and he'd offered to drive us down to the ship next Friday.

I sat with Hassan in my study as the boys got busy warming up in the back and Sudić went to the liquor commission.

"So you're finally leaving," Hassan said. "But you'll be back. You're a man of the revolution, the Third World."

"If I wasn't married, I might stay," I told him. "But what good will it do my family if I die fighting for freedom? In Europe I won't have to take sides. It won't be my war if there is trouble over there."

Hassan smiled. "The head of the viper is here in North America. We can smash world-imperialism and white domination of the non-white world majority right in New York by crushing the head of the viper."

He raised his foot and stomped on an imaginary snake.

"Just think. If we rose up and took over the stockmarket, destroyed all the computers, if riots and revolutions guided by cells of dedicated men suddenly erupted all over North America, co-ordinated with revolts and sabotage all over the world, what could they do? If we smashed the head, the brain, the rest would quiver and die."

He stomped his foot again. "*Allah* will be victorious."

It had been years since Hassan had left his home state just ahead of the Ku-Klux-Klan, an uppity black man fleeing for his life. He had crossed the border into Canada hoping to find refuge, equality, freedom and justice. Instead, like me, he had simply become invisible. Nobody hated him, he just didn't exist. He was treated politely, allowed to eat in any restaurant and have a love affair with any white girl. But he could never aspire to anything beyond his allotted role. After all, there's really no colour problem in Canada, there aren't enough blacks.

The boys in the living room finally got everything organized and started practising. I heard Jimmy singing our latest creation, "In the Stone Bar."

> "*Oy ando birto baruno, ando birto baruno,*
> *Me beshava tai rovava ando birto baruno.*
>
> Oh in the stone bar, in the lonely bar of stone,
> I am sitting there alone, crying in the bar of stone,
> Oh God, why have you punished me,
>   why do you torment me,
> I am sitting here alone, in the lonely bar of stone."

That's us, I thought, sitting forever in the Bistro moaning about our troubles and doing nothing. Sudić returned with his *slivovitz* and we all went into the living room to join the Gypsies.

More guests began to arrive and a mob of Indians appeared carrying cases of beer and gallons of wine into the kitchen.

"We wanna make sure you have enough," Johnnie told me. "It would be a hell of a going away party if we ran out of liquor, wouldn't it?"

Bill arrived with his guitar, and Joe with his common-law wife Margo. Soon the place was crowded and the party really got started. The Gypsy boys played their own Romani music and we danced the old Kalderash dances. Marie did her Arabian dance to an old melody of Jimmy's and I did Baso, the wild dance of defiance. Sudić did

Zorba's dance and later, Hassan and he did their Pathan dance with their respective weapons. An Indian grabbed a replica of a stone war club that I had made and joined in, swinging the club wildly, almost braining some of the guests.

"Yahoo," he cried, shuffling around the other two dancers. "God damned fucking white man, they took our country. This is Indian land, you hear, we Indians and Gypsies, we want our lands back."

Marie started laughing. It reminded her of her own swearing after a few drinks. By now the non-Gypsy guests far outnumbered the Gypsies and they were getting bored with the esoteric Gypsy music.

I went over to Jimmy, the lead musician with his *Bouzouki*.

"All right, James. Let them have it, demolish them, slay them on the spot."

The Gypsies stopped playing their traditional music and broke into a syncopated Gypsy adaptation of the Afro-American beat. This was Gypsy music too, but wild, aberrated and above-all, North American. It told of the big cities, the concrete jungles, the vice, corruption and garbage, of the endless moving in and out of ramshackle houses, the rats, the bedbugs and the cockroaches, the endless trips to the Salvation Army for junk furniture, of the magnificent feasts followed by the hunger and cold of the winter. It tore through the subconscious mind.

The Indians went wild, yelling warcries as they sensed the vibrations. The Blacks followed. Hassan, wearing his fez and leopard skin jacket, was doing a wild dervish dance. Sudić sat on a trunk taking gulps from his bottle of *slivovitz*. He finished his bottle, threw it into the kitchen where it smashed against the wall and he leapt to his feet in a wild Serbian butcher's dance. "Long live Serbia," he yelled. "Down with Churchill and the Anglo-Saxon swine."

Margo, Joe's common-law wife, came over to me.

"Yanko, where's Joe? I can't find him anywhere."

We searched all through the house and finally found him on my bed in the rear of my study behind the curtains. Margo tried to wake him up. She was a simple, horny type.

"Joe," she yelled at him, shaking him. "Joe, wake up you rotten sonovabitch. Don't flake out on me now, Baby. Oh Christ," she moaned.

Jimmy started singing and I heard his voice loud and clear: "Baby come and light my fire, oh yeah, baby come and light my fire."

"You prick," Margo cried, slapping Joe's face. "Wake up you drunken sonovabitch."

"Baby come and light my fire," Jimmy sang on.

"Go tell that Gypsy guy to shut up," Margo screamed. "Joe, you bum. Wake up, I love you, I need you, come on Baby, we gotta get home."

I guessed poor Joe wouldn't be lighting anybody's fire for quite a while. Margo was now lying on the bed rubbing herself against him, her miniskirt up around her waist and her stockinged thighs wrapped around one of Joe's legs.

"Wake up, Baby, come on, let's go home."

Joe didn't wake up and Jimmy kept on singing. Margo finally gave up. "Yanko, that's the third time he's flaked out on my like this week. Is he ever gonna get it! I'll cut off his booze, that's what I'll do."

She left, slamming the door as Jimmy's voice followed her out: "Baby come and light my fire, oh yeah, baby come and light my fire."

I went back into the living room as Jimmy switched to playing a rock and roll beat. Everybody started dancing and hopping around. Some of the guests got on top of the trunks and one of the Gypsy teenagers, Pretzel, a real clown, had found a miniskirt somewhere and had rolled up his pant legs and stuffed two somethings under his sweater. He was gyrating on top of the trunk imitating a go-go dancer. He was a small, skinny runt of a guy who had been nicknamed Pretzel because his mother used to feed him pretzels and potato chips when she was too busy telling fortunes to make him regular meals.

Somebody had turned the lights out and replaced them with a supply of candles. The flames flickered as the couples danced or single dancers did their thing. It looked like hell, Dante's Inferno, and the wild beat was driving them on. Jimmy had been playing steadily for almost two hours now. I walked out to the front lawn to get some fresh air and saw a small figure lying on the grass. One of the Indian girls had passed out there, her glasses lay smashed on the cement sidewalk. I picked her up and carried her into my study and laid her gently on the bed beside the still insensible Joe. I tried to bring her around but she was too far gone. I went to the kitchen to get a wet towel and when I came back, I discovered that Dula had found her. He had pulled her slacks down and had her lying face downwards with her sexy ass across his knees. He was holding a lighted cigarette in his hand, about three inches away from her rump. He had a mad gleam in his eyes.

"Leave her alone," I told him.

He got up and moved away as I rolled her over and started to pull her slacks back up again. She came to and must have figured I had been pulling them down. She threw her arms around me, pulled me down onto the bed and gave me a sexy kiss. Then she realized who I was.

"Not now, Yanko," she giggled. "Your wife might come in."

I heard the sounds of a fight in the back of the house.

"Come on, Dula," I told the sadist. "Help me settle the trouble back there."

We went in the kitchen and found two Indians pummeling the daylights out of each other. Sally the Indian barfly came over to them, her yellow slacks completely stained with wine in a really psychedelic effect.

"Don't fight you fellows," she told them. "We got a swell party going on here. Don't spoil it. Whoopee," she threw the contents of her wine glass up into the air. The Indians shook hands, apologized to each other and started drinking from the same bottle, their arms around each other's shoulders.

Marie appeared.

"Yanko, that old man over there keeps exposing himself to the women. Throw him out."

"What's that?" Sudić asked. "Don't worry, I'll dispose of him."

He went over, grabbed the guy and carried him none too gently through the house and dumped him on the front lawn. I don't know who the guy was or how he got to the party. I'd never seen him before in my life. But the guy was obstinate and Sudić had to throw him out again. This time he took him across the street among the rows of cars in the used car lot. He didn't come back.

The mad beat finally stopped. The Gypsies were tired and I heard Bill playing the guitar and singing his blues to give the boys a rest. The dancers headed for the fridge. I remembered the Indian girl in the front, went back, and found her smooching with some guy who had found his way in there. Joe was back sleeping peacefully. "If you two characters want to make it," I told them, "go somewhere else, this is my bed."

They left and I stood a minute at the window watching the traffic passing in the street. This was the Greek section of Montreal and I could hear the musical voices of the immigrants as they passed outside. There was a bookie next door to me disguised as a travel agent, and a brothel just down the street passing as a Greek social club. Stores, fishmarkets and nightclubs were springing up everywhere in what a few short years ago had been a quiet residential neighbourhood. It was now rapidly turning into a new slum to rival St. Lawrence Main. I thought sadly of the past, of the models I would never make to complete my collection, of my people dying in the slums. Jimmy took over from Bill and started playing softly, singing. I heard the words, in English this time.

"Just tell her I loved her, that I've loved her
        from the very start,
Just tell her that I'm yearnin' to say what's in my heart,
Oh just how forever can you be, the king of a party."

Yes, I thought, how long can you be the king of a party? Yanko, the party-giver and theme director of the Animals of Canada! I smiled sadly, a king was abdicating.

I felt a powerful hand on my shoulder as Joe swung himself down and sat in the armchair beside me. He looked terrible. His hair was sticking out in every direction and his T-shirt was hanging outside his pants. His face was flushed and he was covered in sweat. I gave him a cigarette and lit it for him.

"Tough life," he said.

"Sure is," I agreed. "You'd better get home, Joe, Margo was mad like hell when she couldn't wake you up. She wants you to get over there real fast; she's horny like hell tonight. She threatened to cut off your booze."

"Yeah," he smiled. "I'd better get on over there and fix her up. That's the story of my life, gigolo, three-time loser, a guy who shacks up with big horny broads for his bread and his booze. Wish the hell I could make my own livin'."

"Why don't you?" I asked. "You seem strong and healthy to me."

"Do what?" he asked. "I got no trade, no schoolin'. I started to help my old man with the truck when I was fourteen. I ain't bin much to school. I been in a few times too, got a record."

He showed me his hands, strong, powerful, like the hands of a wrestler or a carnival strongman.

"I keep dreamin' about my hands," he told me. "I see 'em all covered with blood. It scares me. Everytime I see on of them punks sayin' somethin' on T.V. about how this country's so great and everybody's rich an all that crap, I look at my hands and I wanna strangle the cocksucker. I'm dangerous, Yanko. I'm a killer. It's better I stick to my broads and my bottle."

He picked up my rifle hanging over the fireplace, a Mauser 8mm that I'd kept to leave with a very good friend of mine who'd helped me out in the past. It wasn't loaded, thank God. He aimed it out of the window at a passerby, pulled the trigger and I heard the firing pin snap into the empty chamber.

"Lovely baby," he grinned. "Lovely. This is real power, Yanko. With this I could tell them stinkin' bums what I think of them an' their hogwash. This is power. I ain't able to argue like them guys, but with this I could make 'em listen to me and cut 'em down to size fast enough. They'd listen to me then, and my beautiful music, wouldn't they, baby?" He kissed the rifle. "You gotta give me this gun, Yanko, this is a sniper's rifle, I know guns."

It was indeed a sniper's rifle, Deutsche Waffen- und Munitions-fabriken, Berlin 1915.

Bill came in and saw Joe playing with his toy.

"Christ, what are you guys doing, starting your own revolution?"

"I'm not, Bill," I said. "But maybe he is; or maybe he's Canada's version of Lee Harvey Oswald, who knows?"

25

It was Friday, the day we would leave Canada. The phone kept ringing, everybody wanted to say goodby. I decided to go over and see the old man, Demitro, the last patriarch of the Canadian Gypsies. He had tried so hard to save his people from disintegration and extinction in the slums. But like all leaders of off-white minority groups in Canada, he got nowhere. He and I had merely been used by smart alec journalists, radio and T.V. people as a source of interesting or laughable subject matter. Who could take this old guy seriously, with his Panama hat, old fashioned suit, shirt years out of style, white spats and that funny looking homemade badge hanging from his shirt pocket? Our dictionary and its accompanying grammatical study had been long ago completed and now lay unwanted by anybody. It had no value.

But now the old man was dying and they wouldn't have to put up with him much longer. Soon there would be no more talk of Gypsies in Canada's slums, soon "Gypsy Power" would cease to be an issue. The age-old myth of the violins, the caravans, the earrings, blazing campfires and the savage knife fights over the tribal virgin would come back into its own on T.V., in novels and in the movies, while the real Canadian Gypsies were becoming hoodlums, dope addicts, prostitutes and alcoholics following the natural process of the Canadianization of off-white minority groups.

The old man was crippled and could no longer wash, shave himself or light a cigarette. He was living with Jack, one of his sons, at the other end of the city. Charlie had left town with his family and the Gypsies had split up now in a desperate *sauvé qui peut*, hiding like rats in every poor section of town and not congregated into one big cluster like they had been a few years ago around St. Lawrence Main. There were no more fortunetelling parlours and soon they would be denied their last main source of income, dealing in used cars. The lobbyists of the big combines and the gangster-backed syndicates had introduced legislation in Ottawa that would make it virtually impossible for any Gypsy to sell a used car at a profit.

Dula, who was supposed to drive us down to the ship had just been arrested for car theft. I wondered how he'd been able to afford the expensive American model he'd been driving. But Jimmy had offered to take us in his old heap and we had Hassan's station wagon as well.

I took a taxi over to the old man's place. It would be winter soon, he might not survive this one. He was in bed with two large pillows behind his head. He was very weak and tired, but his old eyes still shone. He smiled as I helped him to sit up. He needed a shave badly.

I asked his daughter-in-law for some hot water, shaving soap and a razor. He was sorry to see me leave. He knew that I, perhaps, was the only one who could rally what was left of our people and present their case effectively. But I'd had my fill of being interviewed by idiots. Nobody would listen to me anymore than they would listen to him. I was only some crazy Gypsy who made little boats and he was that senile old duffer talking about the "Rumanians" living in the slums.

The old man talked of the past, and about the time we went in triumph to Ottawa with the dictionary. Kolia's old car had broken down and we spent the night at a motel in the middle of nowhere while Kolia and I repaired the kitchen equipment downstairs to get enough money to fix the car. The Ottawa papers had made a big thing of us in their usual Wasp way, something about "Continent's Romanies Seeking Respectability" and how we were surprised that anyone would take a couple of ex-horse-thieves seriously. But it had been good for the old man, he'd been important again for a while.

I felt sad at leaving him. When he died, the last link with the Gypsy past would go with him except for the manuscripts of folklore, laws, customs and traditions that I had documented. Nobody wanted it here. It was biased, but it might come in handy soon in Europe to light the fire as non-Gypsy authors wrote books telling all about the Gypsies they had never met.

The old man had been in England, a long time ago, before the First World War and he described it for me. "Rich men deal in guineas," he told me. "Tell Mara to charge guineas for her fortunetelling. That way the rich people will come to her. And don't forget," he smiled, "if you need any more words for our dictionary, just let me know. I'll send them to you." But the old man could no longer write.

I finished shaving him and we had a cup of coffee. He asked me to let his relatives in Europe know that he was fine. He had a daughter living in London, running a tea room, and a son somewhere in France. I made a recording of his voice for them on my cassette. I glanced at my watch and saw it was time to leave. I got up and told him I had to go. There were tears in his eyes.

"We tried, Yanko, but we failed them."

"No," I replied, "their own country failed them."

Soon, another of Canada's unwanted sons would die a lonely old man with a broken heart, with his spittoon-pisspot beside his bed and his holy icons and pictures of Jesus Christ and the Virgin on the walls. I stood in the doorway. He sank backwards, slowly, onto his bed, frail and crippled. Only his eyes showed the will to fight on. His blankets were filthy, his pyjamas hadn't been washed for months and his sheets and pillow cases were yellow and covered with stains. I felt sad as I remembered how clean he had kept himself in the whorehouse before he became half-paralysed.

"You'll do all right, Yanko," he told me, still trying to sit up. "You're smart, like your mother, not like these other young Gypsy punks."

He reached into his open briefcase beside his bed, the one he had carried proudly to Ottawa with the dictionary inside and gave me his badge, the one he used to wear over his shirt pocket when he was the *de facto* leader of the Gypsies. It was a blue, green and gold affair with crossed swords, stars, moons, trees and a star of David above the hilts of the swords. It was his symbol of hereditary leadership. I looked at it, then placed it in my pocket as tears came to my eyes. No man could want a worthier medal or award for his service to his people.

"Go with God, Yanko," he told me.

"Stay with God," I replied.

I knew that I would never see him again. He lay quietly on the bed, took a puff from the cigarette held clumsily in his left hand and stretched out his arm full length beside him to relax. It descended

225

slowly, as the old man drifted off into sleep. It finally reached the level of the mattress where it bumped onto the protruding base of the bed and the cigarette was knocked from his fingers. It fell into the spittoon-pisspot below where it went out with a dull splutter.

It would soon disintegrate and its debris would join the other cigarette remains, bits of phlegm and apple cores floating on top of the piss and spittle, just like our people, distintegrating in the slums.

I left and took a taxi home.

Sudić, Hassan and even Etien my separatist friend had arrived and were drinking liquor left over from the party, waiting for me. Soon Jimmy arrived and we loaded the luggage into his old jalopy and Hassan's station wagon. Each of my kids had a favourite toy hanging around his or her neck by a piece of string. István was carrying his toy guitar. I hoped he would one day be a musician like Jimmy.

Jimmy and I had one last drink in the house. I took my glass and threw it against the wall where it smashed into fragments.

"To hell with Canada, Long live Romanestan!"

Jimmy looked at me, only half understanding. He had heard of the proposed Gypsy state, a parallel to Israel, to be set up by the United Nations at the insistence of Gypsy leaders in Europe, educated men like me, who had found that they had no place as Romanies in their countries of birth. But it meant little to Jimmy. His main trouble was finding enough to eat and to keep his instruments and amplifier in shape.

We drove along Sherbrooke Street on the way to the ship. A large mob had gathered around l'Ecole des Beaux-Arts; separatists, students and anarchists were holding a sit-in and a demonstration. They had taken over the school and were defying all comers. The Canadian and Quebec provincial flags had been hauled down and in their place, were flying the red flag of socialism and the black flag of anarchy. The Montreal police were standing around talking and joking with the demonstrators, and unless a major riot erupted they would do little since many of them had exactly the same sentiments.

Yes, Canada might bask in its Anglo-Canadian myth, Toronto the good, Ottawa the bureaucratic, Vancouver the isolated and Halifax the deprived. They were all English-speaking cities. But here was *Le Vieux Montréal*, a wayward child of confederation. She could act like a passionate French whore or a militant fishwife ready to lead the mob to the barricades of revolution.

"*Liberté, fraternité, égalité,*" those cries had once brought a mighty state crashing into ruin and now they were to be heard on Sherbrooke Street in Montreal. *La Révolution des Patriotes* had broken out here over a hundred years ago. It had been suppressed by British troops. But it had smoldered ever since. In France, a Napoleon had emerged to take over the reins. I wondered if Canada could produce a Napoleon.

"*Magnifique,*" Etien was excited as he looked at the students. "*Formidable, on les aura.* It had to come. It's got to be this way, separation, *il faut en finir.*"

Yes, I thought, there must be an end to it somewhere. Will the French-Canadians be allowed to find their own destiny as a separate nation in North America or will they go down in an orgy of blood and terrorism? Who knows? But they can't keep on going the way they are, losing their language, culture and self-respect.

"Stop the car," Etien said. "I want to get out."

Jimmy stopped and he got out, just past the demonstration. He offered me his hand and I took it. We'd played together as kids.

"*Vive le Québec libre!*" he smiled, "*En avant aux barricades.*"

"*Vive le Canada libre,*" I replied. It wasn't quite the same thing.

He ran down the street to join the mob, a little man with curly black hair wearing a dark grey suit and running shoes. Lucky he's wearing running shoes, I thought. If things get too rough he won't have any trouble getting away.

We drove down onto the docks. We'd lost Hassan in the traffic and Jimmy took the wrong turning and ended up in the cargo loading area at the stern of the liner instead of at the passenger embarkation gangway in the middle, a stage higher up. Some burly stevedores rushed over and started putting a girdle around the car.

"What the hell are you guys doing?" Jimmy yelled at them. "My car's not going away, it's my buddy here, Yanko. He's going."

We finally met Marie and the kids along with the rest of the group and went aboard. Visitors were allowed until just before sailing.

Marie stayed in the cabin with the kids unpacking their luggage while the rest of us went into the lounge and had a few drinks. Nobody said very much. George showed up, later, to see us off. Soon it was time for the visitors to leave and we all walked up to the embarcation gangway.

"Good luck," Bill told me, "and remember what I said about your shack and your bananas."

He walked slowly down the gangway, back onto his native soil, the soil he might one day fertilize with his ideas, or his blood.

"*Zbogom*," Sudić smiled, crushing my hand. "I'll see you over there soon." He was planning to visit Europe the following summer.

"May *Allah* go with you, my Gypsy brother," Hassan said, "maybe I'll see you again and maybe I won't. But always remember me and our long talks, wherever you go and whatever you do."

"All the best," George told me, offering his light handshake. "I'll send you a copy of the article when it comes out. And I'll probably be over there soon anyway, I've got some stories to do in London. Maybe I'll do another one on you."

"Like hell," I thought. The guy had just ruined me in Canada and now he was planning to get me over there as well.

"*Zha Devlesa,*" Jimmy said, "and don't forget to save me some of those teas and strumpets, Yanko. I might be over there soon, the Gypsy Beatle."

"Stay with God, James," I smiled. "Maybe you should come over to England. You'd drive those Limey birds wild with your music. They'd demolish you."

He walked down the gangway, a comic little character with long sideburns, moustache, elephant pants and mod jacket.

Marie joined me as the ship moved slowly away from the docks. I watched the group of figures standing there waving at us. What a collection of characters. My friends grew smaller as the ship headed downstream and I took a last, long look at the city where I was born and where I'd spent most of my life, at the Mountain and all the familiar landmarks. We passed under the Jacques Cartier bridge and headed towards Quebec. Marie was crying and I put my arm around her. She looked so sad.

"Soon it'll be as if we never existed. Nobody will know or care who we were and what we tried to do."

I noticed that she had done her hair in braids and was wearing her beaded Indian headband. Did she want to tell the people in Europe that Canada had gotten so bad, even the Indians were leaving?

Two days later, we were on the open sea. Marie and the kids

were eating breakfast and I stood at the stern of the liner and stared at the long, low line of the horizon, my last view of my homeland. I opened the briefcase, took out Paddy's revolver and dropped it over the railing. It landed in the churned-up foam of the propellers and vanished from sight. I had brought some tools, a few books and my typewriter, but somehow I didn't think I would need a gun where I was going.

As I turned to walk back downstairs to join Marie, I whistled,

> "Before me are two roads, which should I take
> The Gypsy road or the non-Gypsy road
> I took the non-Gypsy road but I didn't go far
> I got into big trouble, big trouble
> I ate the leg of a goose and they threw me in jail
> Then I ate the drumstick of a gander and they threw me
> in the dungeon."

Glossary of Romani words and expressions

Afrikaiya (m. pl.), Africans. Gypsies from Africa

ankalavas (v. tr.), to get out, clear our, rescue. *Ankalavas o mobili,* We'll get the car out

arak tu bre, watch out, man. *Arakav-tut,* Take care, Watch out

Ash Devlesa, Stay with God, the Romani farewell, said by the person leaving to the one remaining who then says, *Zha Devlesa,* Go with God

baxt, sastimus, luck and health, a toast, wishing the luck to find work and the health to do it

brashka (f. sing.), female of *brashkoy,* a bullfrog. Roma are mimics and usually give nicknames such as to Kolia's mother-in-law, the *Brashka*

che (int.), what

che chorobia, what vagaries, how funny, how odd

che choromos, what poverty, what misery. *Choromos* means both misery and poverty, being derived from the adjective *choro,* poor or miserable

chi (part.), the negative particle in Romani

Chi dikav kanchi, I don't see anything

chi mai (adv.), never

Chi mai diklem ande viatsa, I never saw such a thing in my life

chorav (v. tr. and intr.), to steal

chuda (adj. and int.), funny, odd, good heavens. *Chuda, che chorobia,* Good heavens, what an odd thing

churi (m. sing.), knife. Lovara variant of Kalderash *shuri*

damfo (m. sing.), steam jacket boiler as used in confectionery factories

de (v. tr. and intr.), to give

De manga Baso, Give me Baso. Baso is an uninhibited dance

Del (m. sing.), God

Devel (m. sing.), God, variant of *Del.* Both are derived from Sanskrit *Deva*

Devla, vocative of *Devel,* used to directly address God

Yoy, Devla, Oh God

Dikes oda baro shero, Look at that show-off. Lovara dialect

diklo (m. sing.), scarf, headscarf, handkerchief. The silk scarf tied on the hair is the symbol of the married Gypsy woman. Unmarried girls wear the hair uncovered

diwano (m. sing.), meeting, discussion

dopo (m. sing.), the axle of a car with one wheel mount sawn off which serves as a portable anvil among the Kalderash Gypsies

dukyaiya (m. pl.), store, Lit. store fronts which serve as for-tunetelling parlours for Gypsy women in North America. Usu-ally the whole family occupies the dwelling, in the rear behind the curtains

Gadji (f. sing.), non-Romani woman. Lovara form of *Gazhi*

Gadjo (m. sing.), non-Romani man

galbi (f. pl.), gold coins, usually worn around the neck on a chain

232

Gazhe (m. pl.), plural of Gazho

Gazho (m. sing.), non-Romani man. This word is derived ultimately from the Sanskrit *garhya* through Prakrit *gajjha* and originally meant "domestic" or person of inferior social status

Gazho si dilo, the non-Gypsy is a fool

Gazhya (f. plur.), non-Gypsy women, plural of *Gazhi*

Gunyeshti (m. plur.), the clan of Gunya, the original patriarch or founder. Romani clan names usually stem patronymically

haide palal, come in the back

Iwon nashentar, They are eloping too

kai (adv.), where

Kai e Tinka? Where is Tinka?

kak (m. sing.), Lit. "uncle", but also refers to a patriarch

kako, vocative of *kak,* the formal address of a patriarch

Kalderash (m. sing.), a Coppersmith Gypsy. A nation of Gypsies. The four great nations of Rom are the Kalderash (Coppersmiths), Lovara (Horse traders), Churara (Sieve makers), and the Machvaiya (People of Machwa)

kana (adv.), when

kana nakadion, when they swallow, absorb

kar (m. sing.), penis

karalo (adj.), lustful

kleshto (m. sing.), tongs

kon (pron.), who

Kon san tu? (sing.), Who are you?

Kon san tume? (plur.), Who are you?

kris (f. sing.), court, trial, justice

Kris Romani, council of Gypsy elders. Romani court which tries Gypsy offenders who have broken one of the ceremonial laws. The Gypsy court has no jurisdiction over crimes against the state which are turned over to the *kris-Gazhikani*, or the non-Gypsy court

kurav (v. tr.), copulate

Kurav tu ando mui, a vile insult. Lit., "I defile your mouth"

Kurav tumare Devlen, I defile your gods. *Devlen* is the accusative plural of Devel

kurva (f. sing.), a woman of immoral character. The Kalderash make no distinction between a professional prostitute or a "good time girl". Any woman who makes love to a man other than her husband is termed *kurva*, so strict is the moral concept of the Gypsies.

lada (f. sing.), trunk, chest

lantso (m. sing.), chain

lavuta (f. sing.), violin

lavutash (m. sing.), violinist

Lovara (m. pl.), one of the Gypsy nations

love (m. pl.), money, monies

Love kuchiaren e bul, Money makes the ass shake, a Romani adage

marime (adj.) ceremonially defiled, unclean. The Roma have three concepts of cleanliness: *wuzho*—clean, *melalo*—dirty with honest dirt, and *marime*—defiled or ceremonially taboo

Martya (f. sing.), the Angel of death

me (pron.), I

Me voliv tu, I love you

mek (v. tr.), to let, allow, permit

Mek len te han muro kar, Let them eat my penis, a curse

merav (v. intr.), to die

mita (f. sing.), bribe, tribute, tax, payola

nai, there is no, there is not, it is not

Nai tut nav Romanes? Have you no Romani name?

O, masculine definite article, always employed with Christian names in Romani. *Kai O Kolia?*—Where is (the) Kolia? or *me sim O Kolia le Valodiasko*—I am Kolia, son of Valodia

Oy, Devla, Hitlerina, so kerdyan amenga? Oh, God, Hitler, what have you done to us?

pakiv (f. sing.), honour, a feast given in honour of one Gypsy or a group of Gypsies by another

pampuritsa (f. sing.), homosexual

panshwardesh dileri, fifty dollars

pechata (f. sing.), mark, badge, emblem

plapono (m. sing.), two eiderdowns sewn together and stuffed with feathers.

pomana (f. sing.), a wake, a period of mourning lasting one year after the death of a Romani adult

pomozhnik (m. sing.), helper, assistant, waiter

priboi (m. sing.), centre punch

rakiya (f. sing.), whisky

rakli (f. sing.), non-Romani girl, a Gypsy girl is called *she*

Rom (m. sing.), a male Gypsy, also a married Gypsy man as opposed to a *shav* or unmarried youth. The word *Rom*, and its derivants, is not connected with the country Romania but with Sanskrit *Rama*, meaning a husband. The Gypsies are an original people and have not taken their generic name from Romania or any other country which came into existence centuries after the Gypsy people

Roma, vocative of *Rom. Sar mai san, Roma?*—How are you, Gypsy?

Romale, vocative plural of Rom

Romanes (f. sing.), the Romani language

Romanestan (f. sing.), a proposed state for the Roma. *Te trayil Romanestan*—May Romanestan yet live. The slogan of the *pralipe* or international nationalist Romani brotherhood

Romania (f. sing.), the code of laws followed by the Gypsy people (pronounced Romaneeya, and not like Romania)

Romanitchel (m. sing.), a Gypsy, especially in Great Britain and France

Romoritsa (f. sing.), an effeminate Gypsy man. *Romoro* is the masculine diminutive of *Rom,*—*itsa* is a feminine diminutive termination. Lit., a little effeminate runt

Ruveshti (m. pl.), the people of the wolf, from *ruv*—a wolf

san, you are

San tu Rom? Are you a Romani?

sap (m. sing.), snake

Sap bianel sap, A snake always gives birth to a snake, a Romani adage

Sar mai san? How are you? the Romani greeting

sarmi (f. pl.), cabbage rolls stuffed with meat, highly spiced

shasto (m. sing.), spree, party, shindig

shave (m. pl.), sons, children, plural of *shav*—son

shel hay hiftawardesh ta pansh dileri, one hundred and seventy-five dollars

si, is, it is, there is

si-ma, I have, Lit. there is to me

si-ma dosta, I have enough

sim, I am

Sintaika (f. sing.), a woman of the Sinti group

Sinto (m. sing.), a man of the Sinti group

si-tu? have you?

Si-tu pasaporto? have you a passport?

si-tut, a variant of *si-tu*

Si-tut love? Have you money?

so, what

So gindis, Mo? What do you think, Dad?

solario (m. sing.), a gold-plated candelabra

te (part.), a word used to introduce optative statements

te del o Del, may God grant

Te del o Del tuka but shave, May God grant you many children

Te xal o rako lengo gortiano, May the crab (cancer) eat their gullets

tomuya (f. sing.), incense

uva (adv.), yes

vitsa (f. sing.), clan

voliv (v. tr.), to love

voliv tu ime, I love you too

wortako (m. sing.), partner, friend, buddy

wortakona, vocative of *wortako*

yoy (int.), oh, ouch, hey. *Yoy, Devla, me merava*—Oh God, I'm
  dying.

zalzairo (m. sing.), acid

zhamutro (m. sing.), son-in-law

zha (v. tr. and intr.), to go

zha Devlesa, see *ash Devlesa*

DUKH — PAIN

BY HEDINA SIJERČIĆ

Hedina Sijerčić's collection of richly evocative poems weave together the author's fleeting joys and enduring tragedies with traditional Romani folklore.

Hedina's poetry is enlightening in its candidness, which shatters the fanciful myth of the mysterious and ever-carefree Roma, replacing it with lyric images of a people living, loving, and dying, not immune to the caprice of the world that surrounds them. It is through such tragedies that the lingering message of these poems has become simply dukh, pain.

RROMANE PARAMICHA:
Stories and Legends of the Gurbeti Roma

BY HEDINA SIJERČIĆ

Rromane Paramicha is a unique collection of folktales and legends that bring alive the rich cultural and religious traditions of the Roma. Hedina Sijerčić, internationally published Romani poet and author, offers us the stories from her childhood with the authenticity of a direct inheritor of oral tradition. This special bilingual edition contains both faithful English translations, as well as the Gurbeti Romani originals of each story, with a selection of Doris Greven's beautiful watercolour illustrations.

Visit www.RomaniFolktales.com for more information.

ROMANI FOLKTALES
(illustrated children's books)

BY HEDINA SIJERČIĆ

A series of beautifully illustrated children's books featuring excerpted Romani folktales from "Rromane Paramicha: Stories and Legends of the Gurbeti Roma".

In each book, Hedina Sijerčić, internationally published Romani Poet and Author, brings us the stories from her childhood with the vivid watercolour painted illustrations of Doris Greven. These special bilingual editions contain both the English versions and the Romani originals of each story.

Visit www.RomaniFolktales.com for more information.

MAGORIA BOOKS
www.MagoriaBooks.com

Coming in 2009 from
MAGORIA BOOKS

HOW LONG IS THE JOURNEY?
(Photography Book)

BY ZSUZSANNA ARDÓ

Magoria Books is proud to bring you Zsuzsanna Ardó's subtle yet communicative photographs of Hungarian Roma living by the river Danube.

Captioned in English, Hungarian, and Romani, the photographer's pictures bring us a myriad candid moments filled with the extraordinary beauty hidden in quotidian Romani life. The exhibition of the same name, from which this book is sourced, was one of several events chosen by the European Commission to mark the European Year of Intercultural Dialogue (2008), and received praise from as far away as India.

MAGORIA BOOKS
www.MagoriaBooks.com

Coming in 2010 from
MAGORIA BOOKS

ME NI DŽANAV TE KAMAV
(tentative title)

BY RUŽDIJA SEJDOVIĆ

Ruždija Sejdović's intimate and symbolically charged love poems bring into keen focus the passion and suffering of both the poet and his people. The delicately crafted verses shift imperceptably from speaking with the voice of one man to echoing the cries of a rising Romani nation still haunted by European demons.

Containing the author's poems in English and Hungarian in addition to the original Romani; this book aims to be a mirror for and a bridge between peoples both kindred and other.

MAGORIA BOOKS
www.MagoriaBooks.com

About Magoria Books

Magoria Books is an independent international publisher specializing in Romani books. Our aim is to provide Romani authors with opportunities to continue to develop and enrich the ever-growing body of Romani literature.

We would therefore like to encourage Romani poets, writers, and activists to approach us with their ideas and proposals. We are particularly interested in folktales, poetry, and other Romani-focused manuscripts, including those written in the Romani language; but are open to considering other relevant materials.

We are also interested in partnerships with translators, community organizations, and foreign publishers to find ways to increase distribution, availability, and impact of existing and upcoming titles.

Write to us at:

Magoria Books
1562 Danforth Avenue #92006
Toronto, ON M4J 5C1
Canada